SIMPLY MING
ONE-POT MEALS

SIMPLY MING
ONE-POT MEALS

QUICK, HEALTHY & AFFORDABLE RECIPES

Ming Tsai & Arthur Boehm

photography by Antonis Achilleos

KYLE BOOKS

For my parents, Iris and Stephen Tsai. You showed me how to eat, travel, cook, love, work and live. Most important, you showed me how to raise children. I'll be a true success if I can give my children what you gave me.

M. T.

For Richard Getke, still the best dining partner.

A. B.

Published in 2010 by Kyle Books, an imprint of Kyle Cathie Ltd. www.kylebooks.com

Distributed by
National Book Network
4501 Forbes Blvd., Suite 200
Lanham, MD 20706
Phone: (800) 462-6420 Fax: (301) 429-5746
custserv@nbnbooks.com

Text © 2010 Ming Tsai
Photography © 2010 Antonis Achilleos
Book design © 2010 Kyle Cathie Limited

Project editor Anja Schmidt
Designer Dirk Kaufman
Photographer Antonis Achilleos
Food styling Ming Tsai
Prop styling Lisa Falso
Copyeditor Janet McDonald
Production Lisa Pinnell and Gemma Jordan

978-1-906868-36-9

Library of Congress Control No: 2010932468

Color reproduction by Chromagraphics
Printed in Singapore by Tien Wah Press

contents

introduction

I love to cook—but like other busy people, I don't always have time. The chef in me aims to make the best, most excitingly delicious food possible; the dad and home cook in me wants those meals to be prepared hassle-free and with minimum cleanup. The solution? The book you're holding—a collection of eighty fabulous dishes that are cooked, start to finish for the most part, in a single pot.

One-pot cooking began for me at home and was introduced during the fourth season of my Public Television show, "Simply Ming." The show's title was chosen because I wanted to present recipes so easy that people would have to try them. That meant using stockpots for sautéing and woks for pasta-cooking and braising, among other time-saving techniques. It soon became clear that I had hit upon a great cooking approach to call my own.

Few home cooks have battalions of utensils, and more people might cook at home more often if the process were simplified. While making great meals on the show from less expensive ingredients like chicken thighs and short ribs, I also saw that anyone could prepare terrific food more affordably. And, I realized that because I always aim to cook as healthily as possible—yogurt instead of cream, lots of veggies and multigrain ingredients—my one-pot recipes could be better for you. Voila! My one-pot cooking system—and, I hope, a one-pot future for you.

Of course, the pot changes depending on the technique used. The seven methods I've chosen—braise, wok, sauté, roast, high temp, soup, and toss—were born for one-pot cooking. They also allow me to present a full range of fabulous dishes, from soups and salads to substantial entrées, that include steamed and flash-fried specialties and everything in between. So much can be achieved in a single pot—you can, for example, prepare a vegetable noodle stir-fry entirely in a wok, from blanching the vegetables and soaking the noodles to their final assembly with other stir-fried ingredients—that you'll marvel at the pot's time-saving versatility. You may even echo my mom, who used to tell me as a young wokking fanatic that the only thing I'd yet to do with that utensil, but probably could, was bathe in it.

No cookbook is gospel. My aim with *Simply Ming One-Pot Meals* is to give you an approach you can make your own so you can create your unique great one-pot dishes. The easier it is to cook, the more likely you will. You won't have to stop Twittering or sending e-mails—in fact, many of the dishes in the book give you more room to do those things. And you'll enjoy sharing great food made by you more often with those you care about.

Exploring technique through my one-pot system—taking underutilized woks and stockpots out for a spin—will also help show you how cooking actually works, so you'll be better at it. The proof, though, is always in the eating, and in that regard, I guarantee serious pleasure.

Peace and Good Eating

glossary of ingredients and techniques

Oils and Vinegars

Grapeseed Oil. Taken from grape seeds, this is my oil of choice for sautéing and wok cooking, as it has a light nutty flavor and relatively high smoke point. I also like to use it in marinades and in dressings, as it emulsifies well. It has a clean, light taste that's superior to that of other vegetable oils. If you have difficulty finding it, canola oil is a good second choice.

Olive Oil. Most people are familiar with this delicious, healthful product of tree-ripened olives. For the recipes in this book I call for extra-virgin olive oil, the result of the fruit's first, cold pressing. Only one-percent acid, it's considered the finest and most flavorful olive oil type. It also ranges widely in color and fruitiness. The greener oils are usually more robust. Experiment with different oils from different countries until you find those you like best.

Toasted Sesame Oil. I refer to the thick, flavorful, brownish oil made from toasted sesame seeds, which is a staple of the Chinese pantry. Unlike refined and almost flavorless sesame oils, which can be used for cooking, this oil is for seasoning only.

Black Vinegar. Similar to balsamic vinegar, this dark, complexly flavored vinegar is made from glutinous rice and malt. It's used in stir-fried dishes, braises, and sauces. Black vinegar hails from the Chinkiang Province of China; it's sometimes labeled "Chinkiang Vinegar."

Rice Wine Vinegar. Most commonly a white to golden vinegar with a delicate taste. It adds a mild acidity to foods. Rice vinegar should be naturally brewed—check labels. I prefer organic brands, such as Wan Ja Shan. Check labels to ensure the vinegar is unseasoned.

Noodles, Rice, and Wrappers

Chow Mein Noodles. Fresh egg and wheat-flour noodles that are used to make chow mein and other dishes. These shouldn't be confused with the crispy noodles that are common in Chinese-American restaurants and that are often sprinkled on stir-fried dishes. Cooked fresh chow mein noodles are sometimes formed into a pancake and fried on both sides.

Mung Bean Noodles. Also known as bean thread and cellophane noodles, these fine, translucent noodles are made from ground mung beans, which also supply bean sprouts for cooking. The noodles are never cooked, but are soaked in hot water until pliable. They're sold dry in bags that range from one ounce to one pound.

Ramen. The name refers to an ingredient—Japanese noodles made from wheat flour, salt, and water—and to commercial noodle-soup kits that contain dehydrated meat, vegetables and flavorings. The noodles, which are sold fresh or dried, usually in Asian markets, are of course the ingredient of interest.

Rice Stick Noodles. One of the large family of fresh and dried rice noodles, this thin flat dried type is widely available in Asian markets.

Rice Vermicelli. Relatively long thin round noodles, these take their English name from the Italian pasta called "little worms." They're sold most often in one-pound bags.

Shanghai Noodles. Sold fresh or dried, these medium-thin egg noodles are usually available in one-pound bags. If unavailable, substitute any thick dried or fresh spaghetti.

Soba Noodles. These earthy buckwheat noodles are probably the most famous of all Japanese pasta, traditionally served in broths or cold with a dipping sauce made with dashi and soy sauce. There are also flavored soba-noodle types; my favorite is cha soba, which has the color and flavor of green tea.

Sushi Rice. A short-grained rice that, when cooked, has a moderately sticky texture that's ideal for making sushi. American-grown sushi rice is widely available; Calrose and Kokhuto Rose are two well-known brands. Sushi rice labeling is sometimes inexact. "Japanese rice, "new rice," or "new variety rice" are "sushi rice" alternatives. The most highly regarded Japanese sushi rice is koshi-hikari. Like risotto rices, it maintains a chewy firmness when cooked, making it perfect for sushi—and risottos. Excellent koshihikari rice is produced domestically.

Wonton Noodles. Thin wheat noodles that take their name from the wonton soup in which they traditionally appear, these are sold fresh and dried.

Wonton Wrappers. Made from flour, eggs, and salt, the skins come in a variety of forms, round and square, thick and thin. Wontons require round skins; square is the choice for making ravioli. In either case, I recommend the thinnest wrappers you can find, which come in packages usually labeled "extra thin." The skins last refrigerated for about a week, and frozen for up to two months. The brand I prefer is Twin Marquis.

Seasonings, Condiments, and Aromatics

Fermented Black Beans. A staple of the Chinese pantry, this pungent ingredient is made from soybeans that are partially decomposed, dried, and usually salted. Sold most often in plastic bags, the beans last indefinitely if stored airtight in a cool, lightless place. The beans should be rinsed before using to remove excess salt.

Five-Spice Powder. A traditional Chinese seasoning blend made usually from equal parts of ground cinnamon, cloves, star anise, fennel seeds and Szechuan peppercorns. It has a fragrant "warm-cool" flavor and an affinity for fatty meats like pork and duck. As the number five is considered significant in Chinese belief, the spice is thought to be healthful.

Fish Sauce. This Southeast Asian staple, called nam pla in Thailand and noc mam in Vietnam, is made from salted and fermented anchovies and is used as often as the Chinese use soy sauce. I prefer the Thai Three Crab brand, which has a clean sea taste and less sweetness than other brands I've tried. Once opened, keep fish sauce in the fridge.

Hoisin Sauce. Sweet and spicy, this traditional soybean-based Chinese ingredient and condiment can also contain sugar, garlic, and vinegar, depending on the brand. Once opened, keep the sauce refrigerated.

Kimchee. This hot, extremely pungent condiment is a staple of the Korean table. Made from fermented vegetables, usually cabbage, kimchee will last indefinitely in its pot or jar, refrigerated.

Korean Chile Pepper Flakes. Known as gochugalu in Korean, this fiery ingredient is made from sun-dried thin peppers. Available in Asian markets, store it airtight, in the refrigerator or freezer.

Mirin. An essential ingredient in Japanese cooking, mirin is rice wine with sugar. It adds delicate sweetness to many dishes and is also used, traditionally, to glaze foods. I recommend hon-mirin, which is naturally brewed and contains natural sugars, rather than aji-mirin, which can contain sweeteners.

Miso. The primary ingredient in the Japanese soup from which it takes its name, miso is a savory paste made from soybeans, rice, barley or brown beans. For the recipes in this book, I call for shiro miso, sometimes called white miso, which is rice-based. Available in cans, jars, and tubs, miso is best stored in the fridge, where it lasts up to three months.

Ponzu. A thin citrus-based sauce commonly used in Japanese cooking, ponzu is traditionally made from mirin, rice vinegar, katsuobushi flakes—dried fermented tuna—and seaweed. I use a naturally brewed wheat-free, tamari-based ponzu made by Wan Ja Shan.

Rock Sugar. A traditional Chinese ingredient, rock sugar has a richer, more mellow flavor than ordinary refined white sugars. As the name suggests, the sugar, which comes in plastic bags, consists of large lumps, which keep indefinitely if stored in a cool dry place. Rock sugar not only sweetens, but gives a sheen to sauces or braising liquids.

Sambal. A fiery Southeast Asian chile-based condiment, the type I call for, and which you're most likely to find, is sambal olek. Made from chiles, vinegar and salt, it contains one of the additives such as garlic or shrimp paste that some other sambal types do have.

Soy Sauce. The essential Chinese seasoning, soy sauce has been used for more than three thousand years. I call for "regular" soy sauce, which is sometimes called light or thin to distinguish it from darker or thicker kinds. Soy sauce is made from a soybean, flour and water mixture, which should be naturally fermented or brewed, rather than synthetically or chemically manufactured. Look for "naturally brewed" on the label and read ingredient listings. Avoid soy sauces that contain hydrolyzed soy protein, corn syrup and caramel color—a sure sign of an ersatz sauce. Japanese Kikkoman soy sauce is a standby, but I prefer an organic brand like Wan Ja Shan.

Tamari Sauce. A traditional soybean-based Japanese seasoning sometimes confused with soy sauce, but darker and richer. I call for wheat-free tamari, sometimes labeled as "organic, wheat-free," which I prefer for its pure good taste. Check ingredient lists on the labels to assure yourself of a wheat-free product. Wan Ja Shan is my brand of choice.

Togarashi. These Japanese chiles are available fresh or dried, and also dried and ground. The latter is the kind required for the recipes in this book and can be found in bottles in Asian markets.

Vegetarian Oyster Sauce. Traditional oyster sauce is a versatile ingredient made from fresh oysters that are cooked and seasoned with soy sauce, salt and spices. Though its somewhat "fishy" taste dissipates in cooking, some people would rather forgo oysters entirely. For them, I recommend vegetarian oyster sauce, which relies on shiitake mushrooms in place of oysters—a reasonable

substitution as both are umami-rich. I prefer the Wan Ja Shan brand.

Yuzu Juice. Squeezed from a sour Japanese citrus fruit used primarily for its rind, the juice has a tart flavor reminiscent of lemon and limes. It is a delicious addition to marinades and dressings.

Other Ingredients

Chicken Sausage. Alternatives to a traditional pork-based sausage can be disappointing. If you buy the right brands, however, you'll be rewarded with a tasty sausage that's sometimes hard to tell from more traditional kinds. I like Aidells, available at retail stores and online.

Coconut Milk. Used traditionally in Southeast Asian rice desserts, curries and shellfish recipes, coconut milk is made by steeping freshly grated coconut in boiling water or milk. I like to use it not only for its flavor, but for its richness; it is a flavorful alternative to heavy cream in many recipes. Coconut milk spoils quickly, so freeze any unused quantity.

Edamame. Young green Japanese soybeans, sold in the pod or shelled in packages, fresh or frozen. The shelled beans add a delicious creamy crunchiness to dishes. Fresh beans are available in Japanese and some other Asian markets usually from June through October.

Blue Ginger Multigrain Brown Rice Chips. My own brand of healthier pack-

aged chips, these are made from brown rice, corn, oats, black sesame seeds and sea salt. They are great for snacking or as a dish accompaniment. They're available nationwide or at www.ming.com.

Panko. These flaky Japanese bread crumbs are used primarily to coat foods for frying. Their texture yields more delicate crusts than their Western counterparts. Panko is available in cellophane bags, in which it lasts indefinitely. Once opened, freeze any unused quantity.

Preserved Lemons. A standard ingredient and condiment of North Africa, these are lemons pickled briefly in a salt and lemon juice mixture. Find them in jars in specialty food shops or online.

Shaoxing Wine. Named after the city of its original manufacture, this preeminent Chinese rice wine has been in production for millenia. Often sold in ceramic containers, the wine is both drunk and used in recipes. Its taste is similar to that of sherry, which can be substituted for it.

Tofu. Prepared from curdled soymilk in a process similar to cheese making, tofu is an ancient Chinese and Japanese product that comes in extra-firm, firm, soft and silken styles. Silken tofu is the most delicate, even if labeled "firm." Protein-rich and low in fat and cholesterol, tofu is extremely nutritious. Though sold fresh in water, it's most commonly available in packages or tubs. Unused portions should be refrigerated in the original container or transferred to water, which should be changed daily.

Techniques and Other Matters

Brining. I always brine pork before cooking it, as well as chicken and turkey for Thanksgiving, and recommend you do too. Brining—soaking meat or poultry in a solution of salt, water, and usually sugar—greatly improves taste and juiciness. It works because the brined item absorbs the solution and retains it during cooking. Brining formulas and directions appear in the recipes.

Deglazing. The process by which a small amount of liquid, often wine, is added to pans or pots in which food has been sautéed and then removed. The liquid is stirred to incorporate the flavorful caramelized crust on the pan's bottom. Other liquids may then be added.

Food Allergies. Work smart. To avoid potential allergic reactions, always clean your cutting board between cutting jobs. If, for example, I'm chopping peanuts or other nuts, I reflexively wash my board before chopping another ingredient on the same surface. Keeping your board clean in this manner also avoids cross-contamination—the transfer of bacteria from raw ingredients to cooked ones. This is especially important when you're having guests whose food sensitivities you—or they—might not know.

Heating the Pan Before Adding Oil. To minimize the possibility of sticking, all my recipes direct that a pan used for browning be heated before adding oil. Following this method, the oil is in contact with the pan for less time and is thus less likely to break down—to become viscous and gummy and thus sticky. Even a bit of broken-down oil can contribute to sticking.

Making Rice. For perfectly cooked rice, I recommend using a rice maker, as millions of Asians do. You get flawless rice every time—and the rice can be held hot in the cooker for up to 8 hours. For making white or brown rice or a combination on top of the stove, I always follow the "Mt. Fuji" method, which involves using your hand to determine how much water is needed in relation to the rice (see 50-50 White and Brown Rice for 4 Servings).

Cooked Rice

50-50 White and Brown Rice for 4 Servings. Rinse 1^1/$_2$ cups of brown rice, and soak it in fresh cold water to cover for 1 hour. Transfer the rice to a medium saucepan.

Place 1^1/$_2$ cups of white rice in a large bowl in the sink. Rinse the rice by filling the bowl with cold water and stirring the rice with a hand. Drain and repeat until the water in the bowl is clear. Transfer the rice to the saucepan.

Flatten the rice with your palm and without removing it, add water until it touches the highest knuckle of your middle finger. Cover and boil over high heat for 10 minutes. Reduce the heat to medium and simmer the rice for 30 minutes. Turn off the heat and let the rice stand, covered, to plump, 20 minutes. Stir gently and serve.

Wild Rice for 3 Cups. Place 1 cup of wild rice in a large bowl in the sink. Rinse the rice by filling the bowl with cold water and stirring the rice with a hand. Drain and repeat until the water in the bowl is clear of any debris. Bring 3 cups water to a boil in a pot, add the rice, reduce the heat, and simmer until the rice is tender, 35 to 55 minutes, depending on the rice. (Check for tenderness periodically.) Stir and serve.

Organic Poultry and Meat. I always recommend that cooks seek out meat and poultry that's certified organic—or is labeled in such a way to indicate that the animal has been raised and slaughtered humanely, without antibiotics or growth-promotants, and on wholesome feed. In the case of poultry, I specify that the birds be free-range. Because of the care given to poultry destined for the kosher table, I also recommend kosher chicken and meat products. The label "naturally raised" indicates that the product has met USDA-established standards for animal well-being and healthfulness. If you can, buy meat and poultry that's been locally raised and processed by small producers, which are usually more conscientious about animal welfare than mass-manufacturers. The payoff for such choosiness is better more healthful, and flavorful, eating.

Roll-Cutting. A traditional Chinese technique that ensures maximum exposed surface area so that cylindrical vegetables like carrots or asparagus cook quickly when stir-fried. Roll-cut vegetables also look pretty. To roll cut, first slice away the stem end on an angle. Roll the vegetable about a quarter turn away from you and slice again at the same angle, about $1^1/_2$ inches further down or to the length of your recipe directs. Continue rolling and slicing until the vegetable has been entirely cut.

Seasoning. I call for frequent seasoning adjustment, as necessary—"correcting" salt, pepper and other seasonings as you cook. To do this, you must taste a dish again and again as it cooks. Repeated tasting is basic to ensuring a delicious result. Please understand that I don't advise overloading a dish with one seasoning or another, but, rather bringing it to its maximum flavor potential through judicial seasoning adjustment.

Skimming Surface Fat with a Ladle. First, using the ladle, remove the larger quantity of surface fat from stocks or soups, transferring the fat to a bowl. Continue to skim; the ladle will now contain less fat and some stock. Allow the fat to rise to the surface and circle the ladle gently over the bowl, permitting the fat to spill into it. Return the remaining stock to the soup. Repeat until all fat is removed.

1

Braising is the original one-pot, "set-it-and-forget-it" technique. To braise, all you do is brown meat or poultry in a pot, add seasonings, aromatics and liquid, and simmer until the main item is done. You then go about your business while the house fills with the best possible cooking smells—throw away those scented candles! A few hours later you've got meltingly tender food.

Easy as they are to do, though, successful braises require great texture-flavor playoffs, and I've made sure all the braises here get them. Luscious, tangy Pork Belly with Jalapeño-Pineapple Salsa and chile-fired Short Ribs with Root Vegetables are delectable examples.

Braising also brings one-pot ease to cooking less expensive cuts of meat, like lamb shanks or oxtail, which require long simmering to be tender. The reward—see Oxtails with Shiitakes and Quinoa—is supremely succulent dining. And braising is flexible; enjoy your braised dish today, then store any leftovers for later. They'll be just as delicious, if not better, the next day.

BRAISE

star anise–ginger "braised" whole chicken

TO DRINK:
A crisp new-world Sauvignon Blanc, like Craggy Range "Te Muna Road" from New Zealand

I often wonder why people cook chicken by any other method than this traditional Chinese one, technically a poach-braise. It delivers beautifully tender, silky meat—and it couldn't be easier. All you do is put a chicken in a pot with stock and flavorings, simmer it until it's partially cooked, then remove it from the heat. The bird finishes cooking in the hot liquid, and emerges perfectly done. The chicken's almost fat-free, having left most of its fat in the stock. Serve with crusty bread.

[Serves 4]

1. In a stockpot or other tall, wide pot or large Dutch oven, combine the celery, carrots, onions, peppercorns, bay leaves, thyme, parsley, star anise, ginger and soy sauce. And the stock and season with salt and pepper.

2. Season the chicken inside and out with salt and pepper. Add the chicken to the pot breast side up. It should be completely covered with stock, but if not, add more.

3. Cover and bring just to a simmer over medium-high heat. Reduce the heat to low and barely simmer for 45 minutes. Turn off the heat and let the pot stand, covered, 30 minutes to 1 hour (the chicken won't cook any further after 30 minutes). Remove the chicken and strain the broth, reserving the vegetables. Carve the chicken and serve with the vegetables and bowls of the broth.

4 celery stalks, cut into 1/2-inch pieces

2 large carrots, peeled and roll-cut into 1/2-inch pieces (see page 13), or cut conventionally

2 large onions, cut into 1/2-inch dice

1 teaspoon black peppercorns

2 bay leaves

2 sprigs fresh thyme

1/4 bunch fresh flat-leaf parsley

2 star anise

2 tablespoons minced ginger

1/2 cup naturally brewed soy sauce or wheat-free tamari sauce

2 quarts fresh chicken stock, or low-sodium canned chicken broth, plus extra, if needed

Kosher salt and freshly ground black pepper

One 5- to 6-pound whole chicken, wing tips folded over the back

TO DRINK:
A fruity, bright Pinot Noir, like
Robert Mondavi Winery or Domaine
Chandon Carneros from California

[Serves 4]

BRAISING SAUCE

4 cups naturally brewed soy sauce

2 cups good red wine

2 pounds rock sugar (see page 10)

3-inch piece of unpeeled ginger, washed
and cut into 1/4-inch slices

3 dried Thai bird chiles

1 medium head garlic, halved
horizontally

1 piece star anise

1 bunch scallions, white and greens parts,
cut into 3-inch lengths

1 medium unpeeled orange,
washed and quartered

2 cinnamon sticks

—

10 duck legs (legs with thighs)

1 large sweet potato, peeled and cut into
1/2-inch slices

1 large daikon, peeled and cut into 1/2-inch
slices

—

50-50 White and Brown Rice (see page 12),
for serving

red-roast duck legs with sweet potatoes and daikon

This incredibly savory braise—and it's a braise, despite its name—takes me back to my childhood, when the scent of simmering red-roast dishes perfumed our house so invitingly. Whole ducks are often used for red-roast dishes, but this one features convenient duck legs—legs with thighs, actually—you can get cheap at Asian markets, from butchers, or online. The sweetness of the potatoes is a perfect foil for the chiles' heat, and the daikon adds crunch. I love this dish served with sambal used as a condiment and a fifty-fifty mixture of brown and white rice.

1. In a large nonreactive pot, combine the braising sauce ingredients. Add 3 cups of water and bring to a boil over high heat. Reduce the heat and simmer until the sugar dissolves, 15 to 20 minutes. Taste and add more soy sauce if the flavor lacks depth, or more water if the sauce seems too seasoned.

2. Add the duck legs and simmer until the meat falls from the bones, about 2 1/2 hours. (*Quick Tip*: You can use a pressure cooker to do this. Cook the duck under pressure for 45 minutes, release the pressure, uncover, and proceed as follows.) Twenty minutes before the duck is cooked, add the potatoes and daikon. Test the potatoes with a fork to make sure they're tender; if not, simmer a bit longer.

3. Remove the legs and vegetables and keep warm. Skim the cooking sauce (a ladle is good for this, see page 13). Divide the duck legs and vegetables among four individual plates, spoon sauce over them, and serve with the rice.

Ming's Tip:
Strain and freeze any extra sauce for future braises of chicken or pork shoulder. The skimmed fat should also be stored, refrigerated. It's great for searing meats or for making scrambled eggs.

oxtail and shiitakes with quinoa

The Chinese love oxtail, a cut that is insufficiently enjoyed in the West. Given a slow braise, oxtail is deliciously unctuous eating. Here, I pair it with shiitakes, for earthiness and texture, and serve it on quinoa, which, if you haven't tried it, is similar in texture to couscous, but is even better for you. When my wife, Polly, is sick she always requests this dish. The Chinese believe oxtail has medicinal properties, but Polly loves it for its soul-satisfying tastiness.

1. Fill a medium bowl with warm water. Add the shiitakes and soak until soft, 30 minutes to 1 hour. Drain, and stem the caps. Quarter the large caps and halve the smaller ones. Set aside.

2. In a large shallow plate, combine the flour and paprika. Season the oxtail pieces with salt and pepper, and dredge in the flour.

3. Heat a stockpot or other tall wide pot over medium heat. Add 2 tablespoons of the oil and swirl to coat the bottom. When the oil is hot, add the oxtail pieces, in batches, if necessary. Cook the oxtail, turning once, until brown, about 8 minutes. Set the oxtail aside.

4. Add the remaining tablespoon of oil to the pot and swirl. When the oil is hot, add the onions and garlic, season with salt and pepper, and sauté until softened, about 3 minutes. Add the wine, deglaze the pot, and reduce the liquid by half, about 2 minutes. Add the reserved mushrooms and the bamboo, season with salt and pepper, and return the oxtail to the pot. Add the soy sauce and enough water to cover the ingredients. Adjust the seasoning, if necessary. Bring to a simmer, cover, and cook over medium-high heat until the meat is falling off the bone, 2 to 3 hours. (**Quick Tip**: cook in a pressure cooker, over medium-high heat, for 1 hour.)

5. Meanwhile, make the quinoa. In a large saucepan, combine the quinoa and 2 cups water. Bring to a boil, reduce the heat, and simmer, stirring occasionally, until the water is absorbed, 12 to 14 minutes.

6. Transfer the quinoa to a large bowl, top with the oxtail mixture, and serve.

TO DRINK:
A big Spanish Rioja, like Atteca Armas Old Vines Garnacha or Borsao Tres Picos Garnacha

[Serves 4]

1 cup dried shiitakes

1½ cups rice flour or brown-rice flour

1 tablespoon paprika

6 large oxtail pieces (6 to 8 ounces each)

Kosher salt and freshly ground black pepper

3 tablespoons grapeseed or canola oil

2 onions, cut into 1-inch dice

2 tablespoons minced garlic

1 cup Shaoxing wine or dry sherry

One 12-ounce can whole bamboo shoots, rinsed well, cut into 1-inch lengths

3 tablespoons naturally brewed soy sauce

1 cup quinoa

Ming's Tip:
When transferring the oxtail from the pot to a serving bowl, be careful to keep the meat and bones together.

aromatic short ribs
with root vegetables

I live in New England, and when the frost builds up on the windows, I make this stick-to-the-ribs (no pun!) dish. It's full of good things—chewy short ribs and sweet root vegetables cooked until their flavors meld into a deeply delicious whole. It's also easy to do: once everything's in the pot, you can forget about the dish until it's time to eat, which, trust me, you'll definitely want to do. Serve this with crusty bread for sauce-mopping.

1. In a large shallow plate, combine the flour and chili powder. Season the ribs with salt and pepper and dredge in the flour mixture.

2. Heat a stockpot or other tall wide pot over medium heat. Add 2 tablespoons of the oil and swirl to coat the bottom. When the oil is hot, shake the excess flour mixture from the ribs, add them to the pot, and cook, turning once, until browned, about 8 minutes. Set the ribs aside.

3. Add the remaining oil to the pot, and swirl to coat the bottom. When the oil is hot, add the onions and garlic and sauté, stirring, about 3 minutes. Add the carrots, celery, celeriac, potato and parsnip. Season with salt and pepper. Add the ribs, soy sauce and enough water to almost cover the ingredients. Taste and adjust the seasoning, if necessary. Cover and cook over medium heat until a paring knife passes through the meat easily, about 3 hours (**Quick Tip**: cook in a pressure cooker, over medium-high heat, for 1 hour.) Transfer the ribs and vegetables to a large bowl and serve.

TO DRINK:
A big red wine, like Aramis "Black Label" Shiraz from Australia

[Serves 4]

1½ cups all-purpose flour

1 tablespoon chili powder

6 single-rib short ribs or 3 double-rib

Kosher salt and freshly ground black pepper

3 tablespoons grapeseed or canola oil

2 onions, cut into 1-inch dice

2 tablespoons minced garlic

1-pound bag carrot nubs

6 celery stalks, split lengthwise and halved if large

1 celeriac (celery root), peeled and cut into 1-inch dice

1 large sweet potato, cut into 1-inch dice

1 large parsnip, roll-cut into 1-inch pieces (see page 13), or cut conventionally

2 tablespoons naturally brewed soy sauce

curry beef with potatoes and onions

TO DRINK:
A California red blend, like Orin Swift The Prisoner or Elderton Ashmead Cabernet Sauvignon

[Serves 4]

2 pounds hanger steak, cut into 1-inch cubes

Kosher salt and freshly ground black pepper

3 tablespoons grapeseed or canola oil

2 large onions, cut into 1-inch dice

1 tablespoon minced ginger

2 tablespoons Madras curry powder

2 large unpeeled russet potatoes, washed, cut into 1-inch dice (see Ming's Tip)

1 quart fresh chicken stock or low-sodium canned chicken broth

1 lemon, cut into wedges

–

50-50 White and Brown Rice (see page 12), for serving

The Japanese love beef curry dishes, which I'm always happy to sample when I'm in Japan. The curries vary in heat and are usually served on rice. My easy version features tasty (and relatively inexpensive) hanger steak, plus onions and potatoes, which absorb the delicious braising liquid. I also call for Madras curry powder, which I find the most reliably—and subtly—flavorful. If you're a curry fan, this quickly made version will do the trick.

1. Season the meat with salt and pepper. Heat a stockpot or other tall wide pot over high heat. Add 2 tablespoons of the oil and swirl to coat the bottom. When the oil is hot, add the beef, in batches if necessary. Sauté until brown on both sides, about 3 minutes. Remove and set aside.

2. Reduce the heat to medium-high and add the remaining tablespoon of oil. Swirl, and when the oil is hot, add the onions, ginger and curry powder. Sauté, stirring, until softened, about 2 minutes. Add the potatoes, the meat and the chicken stock and adjust the seasoning, if necessary. Bring to a simmer, cover, and cook until the meat is spoon-tender, about 1¾ hours.

3. Place the rice on a platter or distribute among four individual plates. Top with the beef and vegetables, garnish with the lemon wedges, and serve.

Ming's Tip:

To dice the potatoes, peel and make a square block of each by trimming the top, bottom, and sides, six cuts in all. Slice the potatoes lengthwise to make planks, pile the planks, and slice lengthwise again. Cut widthwise to dice.

orange-ginger lamb shanks with barley

Every time I eat barley I wonder why it's not more popular. It's delicious—particularly in this hearty dish, where its chewy nuttiness partners with the lamb perfectly. (I won't mention that barley's good for you too—or have I just?) Orange and ginger brighten the dish, which also makes a great presentation. I serve this often for meat-loving friends, and I suggest you do too.

1. In a large pot, cook the barley in an ample quantity of boiling water until tender, about 45 minutes. Using a large strainer, drain the barley, then run cold tap water through it until it's cold. Drain and set aside at room temperature.

2. Meanwhile, season the lamb with salt and pepper. Heat a stockpot over medium-high heat, add the oil, and when hot, add the lamb. Cook on all sides until brown, 8 to 10 minutes. Transfer to a plate.

3. Add the onions, carrots and celery to the pot, season with salt and pepper, and cook, stirring, until the vegetables have softened, about 3 minutes. Add the wine, deglaze the pot, and simmer until the wine is reduced by a quarter, about 8 minutes. Add the orange quarters, soy sauce, brown sugar, ginger and chiles. Return the lamb shanks to the pot and add enough water to barely cover them. Season with salt and pepper. Bring the liquid to a simmer, cover, and reduce the heat to low. Cook until the meat is falling off the bones, about 3 hours.

4. Mound the barley on four individual serving plates or a platter, top with the lamb, spoon the braising liquid over, garnish with the orange slices, and serve.

TO DRINK:
A Bordeaux blend, like Château Cantemerle, Haut Médoc, France

[Serves 4]

2 cups pearl barley

4 lamb shanks, about 4 pounds, preferably from the hind legs

Kosher salt and freshly ground black pepper

2 tablespoons grapeseed or canola oil

2 large onions, roughly chopped

3 carrots, peeled and roughly chopped

3 celery stalks, roughly chopped

1 bottle dry red wine

5 large oranges, 4 quartered, one cut into 1/4-inch slices, for garnish

1/2 cup naturally brewed soy sauce

1 cup dark brown sugar

Four 1/4-inch slices unpeeled ginger, cut lengthwise from a 2- to 4-inch piece

3 dried Thai bird chiles

Ming's Tip:
Try to get hind-leg shanks, which are meatier than those from the forelegs.

garlic osso buco with celeriac

Osso buco—braised veal shank—is a much-loved Italian specialty. My version honors the traditional recipe, including its use of garlic, which I've added copiously (forewarned is forearmed, though cooking mellows its flavor), and is of course tilted toward the East. I've also added celeriac, an underappreciated vegetable, for its special, earthy flavor. This is so good I recommend making a double batch and freezing half for later enjoyment. Crusty bread completes the feast.

1. In a large shallow plate, combine the flour and chili powder. Season the osso buco with salt and pepper. Dredge in the flour mixture and set aside.

2. Heat a stockpot or other tall wide pot over medium heat. Add 2 tablespoons of the oil and swirl to coat the bottom. When the oil is hot, add the osso buco, in batches if necessary, and cook, turning once, until brown, about 8 minutes. Remove the osso buco and set aside.

3. Add the remaining oil, swirl, and when hot, add the onions and garlic. Season with salt and pepper, and sauté until slightly softened, about 1 minute. Add the carrots and celery, season with salt and pepper, and sauté for 1 to 2 minutes. Add the wine and reduce the liquid by half, 2 to 3 minutes. Return the osso buco to the pot, and add the soy sauce, thyme, and enough water to cover the ingredients. Season with salt and pepper, cover, and simmer until the meat falls from the bone, about 3 hours. (*Quick Tip*: cook in a pressure cooker, over medium-high heat, for 1 hour.) Add the celeriac and cook until soft, 15 to 20 minutes. Transfer the vegetables to a platter or four individual plates, top with the osso buco and its sauce, and serve.

TO DRINK:
A big red wine, like Duckhorn Wine Company Paraduxx Zinfandel from California

[Serves 4]

1½ cups all-purpose flour

1 tablespoon chili powder

6 large osso buco (each about 2 inches thick)

Kosher salt and freshly ground black pepper

3 tablespoons grapeseed or canola oil

2 onions, cut into 1-inch dice

20 garlic cloves, sliced thin

1-pound bag carrot nubs

4 celery stalks, cut into 1-inch dice

2 cups red wine

¼ cup naturally brewed soy sauce

3 sprigs fresh thyme

2 large celeriac (celery root), cut into ½-inch dice

Ming's Tip:
I call for six shank sections because people always want seconds.

TO DRINK:
Dow's Ten Year Old Tawny Port

[Serves 4]

1½ cups naturally brewed soy sauce

½ cup dark brown sugar

1 cup of the recommended port (see To Drink) or similar

6 thin slices washed and unpeeled ginger, cut lengthwise from a 2- to 4-inch piece

10 garlic cloves, crushed

2 bunches scallions, white and green parts, 3 pieces thinly sliced, the rest cut into 2-inch lengths

2 cinnamon sticks

Kosher salt and freshly ground black pepper

2 pounds pork belly, cut into 2-inch cubes

2 cups pineapple cut into ¼-inch dice

1 jalapeño, stemmed and minced, seeds included

pork belly with jalapeño-pineapple salsa

Pork belly has become all the rage, but it's long been adored in China, where it's braised until silky. Here, its richness is offset by hot-and-tangy salsa—the perfect accompaniment. Also important to this dish's exceptional flavorfulness is port, whose sweetness enhances that of the meat. And garlic lovers will also rejoice at first taste. This is great served as a starter or as a light entrée.

1. In a stockpot or other tall wide pot, combine the soy sauce, sugar, port, ginger, garlic, scallion lengths and cinnamon sticks. Bring to a simmer over medium heat and season with salt and pepper.

2. Transfer the pork to the pot and add enough water to cover. Simmer, covered, until the pork is cooked through, about 2 hours. (*Quick Tip*: cook in a pressure cooker, over medium-high heat, for 40 minutes.)

3. Meanwhile, make the salsa. In a small bowl, combine the pineapple, sliced scallions and jalapeño and season with salt and pepper. Divide the salsa among four individual serving plates, reserving some for garnishing. Top with the pork, garnish with the remaining salsa, spoon the braising liquid around the pork, and serve.

2

The wok is an amazing cooking tool—*the* one-pot wonder. A utensil of many uses, it's peerless for creating maximally flavored meals in minutes. Folklore has it that the wok originated when Genghis Khan used his inverted helmet as a cooking vessel. It's certain that it was invented in East Asia, where cooking fuel was in short supply and portable cooking tools were obligatory. The wok's "secret" is its round-bottomed shape, which allows very hot seasoned oil to puddle at its base, permitting quick cooking as stir-fried ingredients pass through it repeatedly. This high-heat technique ensures food of vivid color and taste. And your dish is ready in minutes.

A wok was the first pot I ever cooked with. I soon learned it could be used not only for stir-frying, but for braising, steaming—even for pasta cooking. Sometimes combining these methods to make a single dish, recipes in this chapter, such as Green Peppercorn Beef with Asparagus and Rotini and Pork Kimchee with Noodles show how deeply convenient, as well as delicious, wok cooking is.

WOK

chicken and tri-bell pepper chow mein

Growing up, my dad would open the fridge, pull out a few ingredients, and get a chow mein on the table in about fifteen minutes. Bell peppers were almost always a part of these dishes, and I celebrate them—and him—in this quick and easy stir-fry. Chicken, a touch of honey, and fresh lime juice are also key to the deliciousness of this easy dish.

1. Fill a large bowl with water and add ice cubes. In a wok, cook the noodles in abundant boiling salted water until al dente, 3 minutes if fresh, 8 to 10 minutes if dried. Drain and transfer the noodles to the ice water. When cold, drain, transfer to a plate, coat lightly with oil, and set aside.

2. Drain the wok, dry it, and heat over high heat. Add 4 tablespoons of the oil and swirl to coat the pan. When the oil is hot, add the chicken and stir-fry until the chicken is cooked through, about 6 minutes. Transfer the chicken to a plate.

3. Add the remaining 2 tablespoons oil to the wok, swirl, and when hot, add the garlic, ginger and scallions. Stir-fry until soft, about 1 minute. Add the soy sauce, deglaze the wok, and add the honey and lime juice. Simmer until the liquid is reduced by one quarter, about 30 seconds. Return the chicken with any juice in the plate to the wok and add the peppers. Toss, add the noodles, and heat through, about 2 minutes.

4. Transfer to a platter, drizzle with the sesame oil, and serve.

TO DRINK:
An Austrian white wine, like Weingut Huber Alte Setzen Gruner Veltliner

[Serves 4]

1/2 pound fresh or dried chow mein or Shanghai noodles

Kosher salt

6 tablespoons grapeseed or canola oil, plus more for coating the noodles

1 1/2 pounds boneless, skinless chicken breasts, cut across the width into 1/3-inch strips

3 tablespoons minced garlic

2 tablespoons minced ginger

1 bunch scallions, white and green parts, cut into 1-inch lengths

1/4 cup naturally brewed soy sauce

1/4 cup honey

Juice of 2 limes

3 small bell peppers, red, green, and yellow, cut into 1-inch dice

1 tablespoon toasted sesame oil, for drizzling

TO DRINK:
A light microbrew like Magic Hat India Pale Ale

[Serves 4]

1 tablespoon sugar

2 tablespoons sambal

1/4 cup naturally brewed soy sauce

1 tablespoon sesame oil

Zest and juice of 1 lemon

2 pounds dark chicken meat (from the legs and/or thighs), cut into 1/2-inch dice

1/4 cup cornstarch

Kosher salt and freshly ground black pepper

5 tablespoons grapeseed or canola oil

3 tablespoons minced garlic

2 tablespoons minced ginger

1 teaspoon coarsely ground Szechuan peppercorns (see Ming's Tip)

2 cups carrot nubs, sliced 1/4 inch thick

5 celery stalks, cut into 1/2-inch dice

1 cup unsalted roasted peanuts

–

50-50 White and Brown Rice, for serving (see page 12)

Ming's Tip:
Before grinding the Szechuan peppercorns, strain them to ensure that any twigs or small pebbles are removed.

kung pao chicken with house rice

In Szechuan, their place of origin, kung pao dishes always contain chiles and Szechuan peppercorns. American versions, usually made with chicken, omit the peppercorns and always include peanuts. My version has the best of both worlds. I use chicken—flavorful dark meat—plus peanuts and the peppercorns, which the Chinese say produce *mala*, an intriguing, tingly numbness on the tongue. Lemon juice adds bracing acidity to this new old favorite.

1. In a small bowl, combine the sugar, sambal, soy sauce, sesame oil and lemon zest and juice, and stir to dissolve the sugar. Set aside.

2. In a large bowl, combine the chicken and cornstarch, and season with salt and pepper. Toss the chicken to coat it lightly in the cornstarch, remove the chicken to a plate, and set it aside.

3. Heat a wok over high heat. Add 2 tablespoons of the oil and swirl to coat the pan. When the oil is hot, add half the chicken and stir-fry, separating the pieces, until the chicken is cooked through, 3 to 4 minutes. Transfer the chicken to a plate, add 2 more tablespoons of the oil, swirl, and when the oil is hot, stir-fry the remaining chicken. Transfer the chicken to the plate.

4. Add the remaining tablespoon oil and swirl. When the oil is hot, add the garlic, ginger and peppercorns and stir-fry until softened, about 30 seconds. Add the carrots, celery and peanuts and stir-fry until the flavors have combined, about 2 minutes. Add the sugar mixture and, when it simmers, return the chicken to the pan. Stir to combine.

5. Make a bed of the rice on a platter, top with the stir-fry, and serve.

beef, shiitake and broccoli stir-fry

TO DRINK:
A California blend like Cain Cuvee

Stir-fried beef with broccoli is a great Chinese dish that can, however, miss the mark. I've made sure this version is excitingly flavored—and it features shiitakes. This makes a completely satisfying family meal that's quick to put together once the beef has marinated. The natural accompaniment here is my 50-50 White and Brown Rice.

[Serves 4]

1. In a large resalable plastic bag, combine the steak, ginger, garlic, scallions and oyster sauce. Seal the bag and use your hands to distribute the ingredients. Marinate, refrigerated, for at least I hour and up to 5 hours.

2. Meanwhile, separate the broccoli into florets. Cut off their long stems and, using a chef's knife, square the stems so they resemble elongated blocks. Cut the stems lengthwise into 1/4-inch pieces, then stack and cut lengthwise into 1/4-inch strips.

3. Fill a large bowl with water and add ice cubes. Fill a wok with water and bring to a boil. Add the broccoli and blanch for 30 seconds. Drain the broccoli and transfer it to the bowl. When the broccoli is cold, drain and set aside.

4. Heat the wok over high heat. Add 2 tablespoons of the oil, and swirl to coat the pan. When the oil is hot add the mushrooms and stir-fry until soft, about 2 minutes. Season with salt and pepper and transfer the mushrooms to a plate. Add 2 more tablespoons of the oil and swirl to coat the pan. When the oil is hot, add half the beef and stir-fry until medium-rare, 5 to 6 minutes. Using a skimmer, transfer the beef to the plate with the mushrooms. Add the remaining oil, swirl to coat the pan, add the remaining beef, and stir-fry until done. Return the reserved beef and mushrooms to the wok, add the broccoli and stock, and heat through, 2 to 3 minutes. Season with salt and pepper. Using the skimmer, transfer the stir-fry mixture to a platter. Bring the sauce to a simmer, add the cornstarch slurry, and simmer until the sauce is thickened, about 1 minute. Pour over the stir-fry mixture and serve over the rice.

1 pound flank steak, halved lengthwise and cut across the grain into 1/4-inch slices

1 tablespoon minced ginger

2 tablespoons minced garlic

1/2 bunch scallions, white and green parts, cut 1/4 inch thick

1/4 cup oyster sauce

1 large head broccoli

5 tablespoons grapeseed or canola oil

1/2 pound shiitake mushrooms, stemmed and sliced 1/4-inch thick

Kosher salt and freshly ground black pepper

1 cup fresh chicken stock or low-sodium canned chicken broth

1 tablespoon cornstarch mixed with 2 tablespoons water

–

50-50 Brown and White Rice, for serving (see page 12)

Ming's Tip:

If you don't enjoy the flavor of oysters, use vegetarian oyster sauce, now available in many markets as well as Asian groceries.

"French Dip" Orange Beef

TO DRINK:
Yangjing beer from China

This dish consists of orange-marinated-beef hoagies, served with their cooking broth, into which diners dip the sandwiches. Its forebear is Chicago's famous "wet beef" sandwich, which is served "au jus"—thus the title's "French dip." These are fun to make as well as eat, and are perfect for a hungry crowd. You might instruct diners to salute one another before they eat these with a "here's looking at jus," but if you do, don't mention my name.

[Serves 4]

Juice and zest of 2 oranges

1 tablespoon sambal or 1 minced jalapeño

1 bunch scallions, sliced thin, white and green parts separated

1 tablespoon minced ginger

2 shallots, sliced thin

1½-pound hanger steak, any silverskin removed, and sliced as thin as possible

4 tablespoons grapeseed or canola oil

2 cups fresh beef stock, fresh chicken stock, or low-sodium canned broth

1 tablespoon naturally brewed soy sauce, if needed

Kosher salt and freshly ground black pepper

—

4 soft hoagie buns

1 large tomato, or 3 roma tomatoes, sliced ¼ inch thick

1 small head iceberg lettuce, shredded

1. In a medium bowl, combine the orange juice, sambal, scallion whites, ginger and shallots. Add the beef, stir to coat the slices, and marinate for 15 minutes.

2. Drain the beef, and reserve the marinade. Heat a wok over high heat. Add 2 tablespoons of the oil and swirl to coat the pan. When the oil is hot, add half the beef and stir-fry until cooked through, 4 to 5 minutes. Transfer the beef to a plate. Add the remaining two tablespoons oil to the wok, swirl, stir-fry the remaining beef, and transfer to the plate.

3. Add the stock and reserved marinade. Add the soy sauce if the stock is unsalted or low-sodium. Add the orange zest and scallion greens, season with salt and pepper, and bring to a boil. Transfer the broth to four individual bowls.

4. To make the hoagies, split the rolls in half. On the bottom halves place the tomato slices and top with the lettuce, then the beef. Cover with the bun tops, and serve with the broth bowls for dipping the hoagies into.

Ming's Tip:

To slice the beef easily, freeze it first for two hours. My Blue Ginger Multigrain Brown Rice Chips (see page 11) are the natural accompaniment here.

green peppercorn beef with asparagus and rotini

Corkscrew-shaped rotini are awesome sauce-trappers, one reason I love them. Here, the pasta is paired with asparagus—a vegetable that gives its flavor-all when stir-fried—beef and green peppercorns. Steak with black peppercorns is a traditional match, but green peppercorns have a fresher yet pungent flavor that goes beautifully with wok-cooked beef.

1. Fill a large bowl with water and add ice cubes. In a wok, cook the asparagus in abundant boiling salted water until tender-crisp, 1 to 2 minutes. Transfer to the ice water with a skimmer, and when cold, drain. Cut the asparagus into 2-inch lengths, and set aside.

2. Add more ice cubes to the bowl, if necessary. Return the water in the wok to a boil and cook the pasta until al dente, about 11 minutes. Transfer to the ice water and when cold, drain and set aside.

3. Drain and dry the wok and heat it over high heat. Add 2 tablespoons of the oil and swirl to coat the bottom. When the oil is hot, add half the beef and stir-fry until rare, 3 to 4 minutes. Transfer to a plate. Add 2 more tablespoons of the oil, swirl, stir-fry the remaining beef, and transfer to the plate.

4. Add the remaining tablespoon oil to the wok, swirl, and when the oil is hot, add the garlic, peppercorns and scallions. Season with salt and pepper and stir-fry until soft, about 2 minutes. Return the beef to the wok, add the asparagus, rotini and stock, and stir-fry until heated through, 3 to 4 minutes. Add the soy sauce and stir to blend. Adjust the seasoning, if necessary, and serve in four individual pasta dishes.

TO DRINK:
A spicy Shiraz, like Kangarilla Road Shiraz/Viognier from Australia

[Serves 4]

1 pound thin asparagus, ends trimmed

Kosher salt

1/2 pound rotini pasta

5 tablespoons grapeseed or canola oil

1 1/2 pounds flank steak, any silverskin removed, sliced on the bias, 1/4 inch thick

5 garlic cloves, sliced thin

2 tablespoons crushed green peppercorns

1 bunch scallions, white and green parts, sliced thin

Freshly ground black pepper

1/2 cup fresh chicken stock or low-sodium canned chicken broth

2 tablespoons naturally brewed soy sauce

Ming's Tip:

To crush the peppercorns, arrange in a circle on a cutting board, and crush with the back of a heavy pan.

TO DRINK:
Trimbach Riesling

[Serves 4]

2 tablespoons naturally brewed soy sauce

1 tablespoon minced garlic

2 medium pork tenderloins (about
2 pounds), any silverskin removed, cut
into ¼-inch slices

½ pound mung bean noodles

3 tablespoons grapeseed or canola oil

Kosher salt and freshly ground black pepper

1 medium red onion, halved lengthwise
and sliced thin

2 cups cabbage kimchee

1 small zucchini, sliced as thin as possible

1 cup fresh chicken stock or low-sodium
canned chicken broth

½ teaspoon Korean chile pepper flakes
or ancho chile powder

pork kimchee
with noodles

Stir-fried pork with kimchee is a beloved Korean dish. Kimchee, made usually from fermented cabbage, is wonderfully pungent—though I don't recommend playing spin-the-bottle after eating it. In addition to these ingredients, I've included satisfying mung bean noodles and zucchini. This is a terrific dish—real excitement on the plate.

1. In a medium bowl, combine the soy sauce and garlic. Add the pork, toss, and marinate, refrigerated, for 30 minutes.

2. Meanwhile, place the noodles in a wok and fill with hot water to cover. When the noodles have softened, after about 10 minutes, drain and transfer to a bowl.

3. Dry the wok and heat it over high heat. Add 2 tablespoons of the oil and swirl to coat the pan. When the oil is hot, add the pork, season with salt and pepper, and stir-fry until just cooked through, 6 to 8 minutes. Transfer the pork to a plate, add the remaining tablespoon oil to the wok, and swirl to coat the pan. When the oil is hot, add the onion and stir-fry until soft, about 2 minutes. Add the kimchee and zucchini and season with salt and pepper. Add the pork, stock and the noodles, mix, and heat through, 1 to 2 minutes.

4. Transfer to four individual serving bowls, garnish with the chile pepper flakes, and serve.

Ming's Tip:

A mandoline makes the job of slicing the zucchini, among other cutting chores, a snap. If you don't own one, I suggest a ceramic model like the one Kyocera makes, which does the job quickly and is also inexpensive.

gingered pork with leeks

TO DRINK:
Chilled Mulderbosch Cabernet Sauvignon Rosé from South Africa

[Serves 4]

2 tablespoons organic Worcestershire sauce

1 tablespoon minced garlic

1 tablespoon sesame oil

2 serrano chiles, 1 minced, 1 sliced thin for garnish

2 tablespoons naturally brewed soy sauce

1 pound pork loin, sliced as thin as possible

3 tablespoons grapeseed or canola oil

2 tablespoons peeled finely sliced ginger

3 large leeks, white parts, halved, cut into strips, washed and dried (see Ming's Tip)

Kosher salt and freshly ground black pepper

–

50-50 White and Brown Rice, for serving (see page 12)

I fell in love with leeks the first time I visited Paris. Wok-cooked, this wonderful member of the onion family has a bite and sweetness that other cooking methods don't deliver. Pork is a natural companion, as its subtle sweetness enhances that of the leeks—and vice versa. Heat from ginger and chile helps to make this a completely winning dish.

1. In a medium bowl, combine the Worcestershire, garlic, sesame oil, minced chile, and soy sauce, and blend. Add the pork, stir gently to coat it, and marinate for 30 minutes.

2. Drain the pork. Heat a wok over high heat. Add 2 tablespoons of the oil and swirl to coat the pan. When the oil is hot, add the pork and stir-fry until cooked through, 5 to 6 minutes. Transfer the pork to a plate and set aside.

3. Add the remaining oil to the wok, swirl, and when the oil is hot, add the ginger. Stir-fry 20 seconds, add the leeks, and season with salt and pepper. Stir-fry until the leeks are soft, about 2 minutes. Return the pork to the wok and heat through, 2 to 3 minutes.

4. Transfer to a serving bowl, garnish with the chile slices, and serve with the rice.

Ming's Tip:

To cut the leeks into thin strips easily, halve the white parts lengthwise and discard about one third of the interior. Flatten against your cutting surface and slice. Fill the bowl of a salad spinner with water, add the leeks, and swish with your hands to remove any sand. Transfer the leeks to the spinner insert, dump out the water, and rinse the bowl well. Spin the leeks dry.

scallop and bacon fettuccine

I can eat scallops wrapped in bacon like peanuts. The combination of sweet and salty is perfect—and even better when paired with creamy fettuccine. As rich as all this might sound, I've made sure to keep the calories under control, and the dish non-cloying, by using yogurt in place of cream and adding spinach for its fresh green note.

1. Fill a large bowl with water and add ice cubes. In a wok, cook the pasta in abundant boiling salted water until al dente, about 3 minutes if fresh, 11 minutes if dry. Drain the pasta and transfer it to the bowl. When cold, drain the pasta and transfer it to a medium bowl. Coat the pasta lightly with oil and set it aside.

2. Line a plate with paper towels. Heat the wok over medium heat. Add the bacon and stir-fry until crisp, about 4 to 5 minutes. Using a skimmer, transfer the bacon to the plate.

3. Wipe out the wok and heat it over medium-high heat. Add the 1 tablespoon oil and swirl to coat the pan. When the oil is hot, add the onions and ginger and stir-fry until soft, about 3 minutes. Add the scallops and stir-fry until almost cooked through, 1 minute. Add the wine and stock, deglaze, and allow the liquid to reduce by one quarter, 1 to 2 minutes. Add the yogurt, all but 1 tablespoon of the reserved bacon, the pasta, spinach and the chopped parsley. Toss gently to blend, and heat through, about 2 minutes. Season with salt and pepper. Divide among four individual plates or pasta bowls, garnish with the parsley leaves and reserved bacon, and serve.

TO DRINK:
An Italian rosé, like Heitz Wine Cellars Grignolino

[Serves 4]

1/2 pound fettuccine, fresh or dried

Kosher salt

1 tablespoon extra-virgin olive oil, plus more for coating the pasta

1/4 pound sliced bacon, cut into 1/4-inch pieces

1 medium red onion, cut in 1/4-inch dice

1 tablespoon minced ginger

1 pound medium (U-20) scallops, any muscles removed, halved

1/2 cup dry white wine

1/2 cup fresh chicken stock or low-sodium canned chicken broth

1/2 cup Greek yogurt

1/2 pound baby spinach leaves

2 tablespoons chopped fresh flat-leaf parsley, plus leaves for garnish

Freshly ground black pepper

Ming's Tip:
You can make this with whole-wheat fettuccine, which adds its own flavorful nuttiness.

TO DRINK:
*An off-dry Oregon Riesling, like
A to Z*

[Serves 4]

¼ cup cornmeal

2 pounds clams, such as Manila or littleneck

1 medium avocado, the flesh cut into ½-inch
dice (see Ming's Tip)

Juice of I lime

Kosher salt and freshly ground black pepper

3 tablespoons grapeseed or canola oil

½ pound ground pork

3 tablespoons minced garlic

2 tablespoons minced ginger

1 bunch scallions, white and green parts,
cut into 1-inch lengths (halve the white parts
if large)

2 tablespoons sambal

2 tablespoons naturally brewed soy sauce

2 tablespoons naturally brewed rice vinegar

2 tablespoons honey

1 medium jicama, peeled and cut into
½-inch dice

1 medium red bell pepper, cut into ¼-inch
dice (see Ming's Tip)

clams with pork and jicama

I based this dish on the great Portuguese favorite, *alentejana*—braised pork with clams. Wok cooking really brings out the best in this traditional pairing, which is enhanced by jicama and buttery avocado. I love translating a dish from one culture to another, which can really make the tried-and-true sing.

1. Fill a large bowl with water. Add the cornmeal, stir, and add the clams. Let the clams purge for at least 1 hour and up to 3. Rinse, drain the clams well, and set aside. Discard the water and cornmeal.

2. Meanwhile, place the avocado in a small bowl. Add the lime juice, season with salt and pepper, and toss. Cover with plastic wrap and set aside.

3. Heat a wok over high heat. Add 1 tablespoon of the oil and swirl to coat the pan. When the oil is hot, add the pork, season with salt and pepper, and stir-fry, breaking up the pork, until brown, 6 to 8 minutes. Transfer the pork to a plate.

4. Add the remaining 2 tablespoons oil to the wok and swirl to coat. Add the clams, and stir-fry until the clams start to open, about 4 minutes. Add the garlic, ginger, scallions, sambal, soy sauce, vinegar and honey. Return the pork to the wok, add the jicama and bell pepper, cover, and sweat until the clams open fully, about 4 minutes. Discard any clams that haven't opened.

5. Transfer the stir-fry to a platter, sprinkle with the avocado, and serve.

Ming's Tip:

To dice an avocado, halve it lengthwise, remove the pit, and separate the flesh from the peel. Slice the flesh parallel to your cutting surface, cut the stacked slices lengthwise, then cut crosswise to dice. To dice a bell pepper easily, first cut away both ends. Cut downward into the pepper on one long side and "peel" away its flesh by rolling the pepper while you cut. You'll have separated the useable part of the pepper from its core and seeds. Halve the useable part and stack the halves. Slice lengthwise, then cut crosswise to dice.

black-bean scallops and zucchini

TO DRINK:
Yanjing beer from China

In China, scallops with black beans is second in popularity to black beans and clams. For my money, the first combo is the best, as the scallops' sweetness makes a perfect foil for the beans' salty savor. This easy dish also features zucchini, an underused vegetable that has great color and texture and is also inexpensive. It's made quickly, too.

1. Heat a wok over medium-high heat. Add the oil and swirl to coat the bottom. When the oil is hot, add the black beans, garlic and scallion whites. Season with salt and pepper and sauté until softened, about 1 minute. Add the scallops and zucchini and sauté until the scallops are just cooked through, 5 to 6 minutes.

2. Add the butter and adjust the seasoning, if necessary. Add the scallion greens and stir to combine.

3. Transfer the stir-fry to four individual serving plates and serve with the rice on the side.

[Serves 4]

2 tablespoons grapeseed or canola oil

2 tablespoons minced fermented black beans

1 tablespoon minced garlic

1 bunch scallions, thinly sliced, white and green parts separated

Kosher salt and freshly ground black pepper

1 pound medium (U-20) scallops, muscles removed, halved

2 cups 1/4-inch sliced zucchini

2 tablespoons unsalted butter

–

50-50 White and Brown Rice, for serving (see page 12)

black-pepper sake mussels with granny smith apples

TO DRINK:
An Alsatian Riesling like Trimbach

Apples may seem an odd mate for mussels, but the pairing is inspired, if I say so myself. The apples' tart-sweetness plays beautifully against the sweetness of the mussels—and sake, which can have a faint apple nuance, furthers the flavor-play. Black pepper, generously included, adds resonance. This is another quick dish.

1. Heat a wok over high heat. Add the oil and swirl to coat the pan. When the oil is hot, add the garlic, shallots and coarse black pepper and stir-fry for 30 seconds. Add the mussels, and season with salt and pepper. Add the sake, deglaze, and cover the wok. When the mussels have begun to open, after about 3 minutes, add the apples and butter. (Discard any mussels that haven't opened.)

2. Continue to cook until the flavors have combined, about 2 minutes. Adjust the seasoning, if necessary. Transfer to a large serving bowl, sprinkle with the togarashi, and serve.

[Serves 4]

2 tablespoons grapeseed or canola oil

1 tablespoon minced garlic

3 large shallots, sliced thin

1 tablespoon coarsely ground black pepper

2 pounds mussels, preferably Prince Edward Island, cleaned and beards removed

Kosher salt and freshly ground black pepper

1/2 cup sake

2 Granny Smith apples, unpeeled, cored, and cut into fine strips

4 tablespoons (1/2 stick) unsalted butter

Pinches of togarashi or other hot pepper, for garnish

TO DRINK:
A Chenin Blanc, like Spier Discover
Steen from South Africa

[Serves 4]

1/4 cup cornmeal

2 pounds small clams, such as Manila,
or cockles

1 tablespoon grapeseed or canola oil

2 slices bacon, diced fine

4 garlic cloves, sliced thin

1 large jalapeño, preferably red, unseeded
and sliced thin

2 large leeks, white parts, halved, cut into
very thin strips, washed, and dried (see
Ming's Tip, page 47)

Kosher salt and freshly ground black pepper

3/4 cup mirin

1/4 cup Greek yogurt

Juice of 1 lemon

mirin clams and leeks

Although we've done a very successful version of this dish at Blue Ginger, I keep reinventing it. I get very involved with flavor matching—especially with the way mirin's sweetness complements that of leeks so beautifully and how both do wonders for clams. This time around I've added bacon and, I think, created a winner.

1. Fill a large bowl with water. Add the cornmeal, stir, and add the clams. Let the clams purge for at least 1 hour and up to 3. Rinse, drain the clams well, and set aside. Discard the water and cornmeal.

2. Heat a wok over medium-high heat. Add the oil and swirl to coat the pan. When the oil is hot, add the bacon and stir-fry until the bacon is crisp, about 3 minutes. Pour off all but 1 tablespoons of the fat. Add the clams and stir-fry until they start to open, about 2 minutes.

3. Add the garlic, jalapeño and leeks, and stir-fry until softened, about 3 minutes. Season with salt and pepper. Add the mirin, deglaze, cover, and cook until all the clams have opened, 4 to 6 minutes. Discard any clams that remain unopened. Add the yogurt and lemon juice and stir. Transfer to a platter or four large serving bowls and serve.

Ming's Tip:
This dish really requires crusty bread for sopping, as no one will want to miss a bit if the sauce.

tamari tofu stir-fry with rice noodles

TO DRINK:
Robert Mondavi Riesling

I love rice noodles in all their forms. This dish features rice vermicelli, which are long and thin and have a wonderfully chewy texture. Tofu, the dish's centerpiece, receives ample flavoring from the tamari, which also enhances the broccoli's sweetness—and hot sauce adds its kick. Tofu skeptics will be instantly won over by this delectable dish.

[Serves 4]

1. In a medium bowl, combine the tamari, hot sauce, garlic and ginger. Add the tofu, stir gently, and marinate for 15 minutes.

2. Meanwhile, fill a large bowl with water and add ice cubes. Bring abundant salted water to a boil in a wok. Add the broccoli, blanch for 30 seconds, and using a large strainer, transfer the broccoli to the ice water. When the broccoli is cold, drain and set aside. Don't drain the wok water.

3. Add more ice cubes to the bowl, if necessary. Add 2 cups cold water to the wok. Add the noodles and allow them to soften, about 10 minutes. Using the strainer, transfer the noodles to the ice water, and when cold, drain them and set aside.

4. Drain the water from the wok and dry it. Heat it over high heat, add the oil, and swirl to coat the pan. When the oil is hot, add the scallion whites and stir-fry until soft, about 30 seconds. Add the tofu with its marinade and stir-fry until heated through, about 2 minutes. Return the broccoli and noodles to the wok, toss gently to combine, and heat through, about 2 minutes. Season with salt and pepper.

5. Transfer the stir-fry to a four individual serving bowls, garnish with the scallion greens, and serve with the lemon wedges, if using, for squeezing over the dish.

¼ cup wheat-free tamari sauce

1 to 2 tablespoons hot sauce

1 tablespoon minced garlic

1 tablespoon minced ginger

One 14-ounce package firm tofu, cut into ½-inch dice

Kosher salt

1 head broccoli, florets separated, stems peeled, squared, and cut into thin strips

One 8-ounce package rice vermicelli

2 tablespoons grapeseed or canola oil

1 bunch scallions, sliced thin, white and green parts separated

Freshly ground black pepper

1 lemon, cut into wedges (optional)

cauliflower and maitake mushroom stir-fry

TO DRINK:
A French rosé, like Couly–Dutheil René Chinon

[Serves 4]

Kosher salt

1 small head cauliflower, separated into florets

2 tablespoons unsalted butter

1 cup panko (Japanese bread crumbs)

2 tablespoons grapeseed or canola oil

2 tablespoons minced garlic

1 tablespoon minced ginger

1 head maitake (hen of the woods) mushrooms, stem removed, trimmed, peeled (see Ming's Tip) and sliced ¼ inch thick, or 2 cups shiitake caps, quartered if large, halved if medium

¼ cup vegetarian oyster sauce

Zest and juice of 1 lemon

Freshly ground black pepper

50-50 White and Brown Rice, for serving (see page 12)

1 tablespoon finely sliced chives, for garnish

Maitake mushrooms—also known as "hen of the woods"—are the king of mushrooms. I love their unique, earthy taste—and they're exceptionally good for you. In this simple stir-fry, the mushroom flavor comes through loud and clear. Cauliflower has something of a dubious rep due to indifferent preparation, but in this dish it's subtly delicious.

1. Fill a large bowl with water and ice cubes. Bring abundant salted water to a boil in a wok. Add the cauliflower and blanch for 30 seconds, drain, and transfer it to the ice water. When the cauliflower is cold, drain it, transfer it to a plate, and set aside.

2. Dry the wok, add the butter, and heat it over high heat. When the butter has melted, add the panko and stir-fry gently until the panko is golden brown, about 1 minute. Watch carefully to avoid burning. Transfer the panko to a medium bowl.

3. Wipe out the wok, and heat over high heat. Add the oil and swirl to coat the pan. When the oil is hot, add the garlic, ginger and maitake and stir-fry until softened, about 2 minutes. Add the cauliflower, oyster sauce and lemon zest and juice. Season with salt and pepper and stir to heat through, 2 to 3 minutes.

4. Make a bed of the rice on a platter, or transfer to four individual serving bowls, and top with the stir-fry. Sprinkle with the panko, garnish with the chives, and serve.

Ming's Tip:
To peel the maitake stem, use a sharp paring knife.

3

Traditional sautéing involves searing ingredients in an oil-coated skillet. These are tossed or stirred as they brown. I applaud the tried-and true, but why limit sautéing to one shallow utensil? My one-pot method introduces pot sautéing—searing in a tall wide pot into which other ingredients are added to create a delicious "meal-in-one." Dishes like Black Bean Orecchiette with Spicy Pork and Broccoli and Seared Curried Butterfish with Warm Olive Chutney are based on this easy, innovative—and spatter-free—approach.

I also take advantage of traditional sautéing to create exciting recastings of old favorites—like Asian Sloppy Joes—as well as other "innovations," such as Potato-Crusted Halibut with Shaved Fennel Salad, and Loin Lamb Chops with Eggplant and Lemongrass Tzatziki. Sautéing has never been considered a particularly versatile method, but following my one-pot approach, it is.

SAUTÉ

chicken meatballs with penne and tomato sauce

TO DRINK:
A good Italian country red, like Altesino Rosso di Moutalcino

[Serves 4]

1 pound penne

Kosher salt

4 tablespoons extra-virgin olive oil, plus extra for coating the pasta

1 large onion, minced

1 tablespoon minced garlic

½ cup panko (Japanese bread crumbs)

1 pound ground chicken

2 large eggs

Freshly ground black pepper

1 bunch scallions, white and green parts, sliced thin

One 32-ounce jar best-quality tomato sauce

20 Thai basil leaves or regular basil leaves

Everyone loves meatballs and pasta. The meatballs in this dish are made with chicken, which is every bit as good as the beef-based kind, not to mention better for you; penne, the quill-shaped pasta, has great mouthfeel and traps sauce beautifully. Because chicken is a lean meat, I add panko—Japanese bread crumbs—to the meatball mixture so everything coheres. And to make this dish especially easy, I call for store-bought tomato sauce as a base for the pasta accompaniment. Get your favorite brand and you're in business.

1. Fill a large bowl with water and add ice cubes. In a stockpot or other tall wide pot, cook the pasta in abundant salted boiling water until al dente, about 11 minutes. Using a large strainer, drain the pasta, and transfer in the strainer to the ice water. When the pasta is cold, drain and transfer to a medium bowl. Drizzle in enough oil to coat it lightly and toss. Set aside.

2. Heat the pot over medium-high heat. Add 2 tablespoons of the oil and swirl to coat the bottom. When the oil is hot, add the onions and garlic and sauté until brown, about 6 minutes. Transfer to a large bowl. Reserve the pot.

3. When the onion mixture is cool, add the panko, chicken, and eggs. Season with salt and pepper. Blend lightly, and test the seasoning by sautéing or microwaving a bit of it. Adjust the seasoning, if necessary. With wet hands form the mixture into meatballs the size of Ping-Pong balls.

4. Heat the pot over high heat. Add the remaining 2 tablespoons oil and swirl to coat the bottom. When the oil is hot, and working in batches, if necessary, add the meatballs. Sauté the meatballs on all sides until brown, 4 to 5 minutes. Add the scallions, tomato sauce and basil, reduce the heat to medium-low, and simmer to blend the flavors, about 10 minutes. Add the pasta and mix well. Season with salt and pepper and serve.

loin lamb chops with eggplant and lemongrass tzatziki

The Greeks may not have been the first to pair lamb and yogurt, but they've done a bang-up job with the match. Tzatziki is the delicious yogurt medium that, in my rendering, includes lemongrass. The chops are served on eggplant slices, which sop up their delicious juice. This is a perfect summertime dish, great for outdoor grilling; but it's equally satisfying year round.

1. Peel the cucumber and quarter it lengthwise. Place it in a colander, sprinkle generously with salt, and allow to drain for 30 minutes. Rinse the cucumber and cut into ¼-inch dice.

2. Meanwhile, peel the eggplant lengthwise in ½-inch strips "zebra-style," leaving a ½-inch strip of skin between each peel. Cut the eggplant widthwise into eight 1-inch slices. Set aside.

3. Make the tzatziki: Heat a large sauté pan over high heat. Add 1 tablespoon of the oil and swirl to coat the bottom. When the oil is hot, add the lemongrass and garlic and sauté, stirring, until soft, about 3 minutes. Don't allow the mixture to color. Transfer to a small bowl and when cool, add the yogurt, cucumber, mint, and lemon juice. Mix well, season with salt and pepper, and refrigerate.

4. Season the lamb chops with salt and pepper. Heat the pan over medium-high heat. Add the remaining 2 tablespoons of the oil and swirl to coat the bottom. When the oil is hot, add the lamb chops and sauté until brown on both sides, about 10 minutes. Transfer to a plate and set aside.

5. Meanwhile, brush the eggplant on both sides with oil and season with salt and pepper. Working in batches, if necessary, add the eggplant to the pan and sauté, turning once, until the slices are lightly colored, 4 to 6 minutes. Arrange the eggplant on a platter and top each slice with a chop. Serve with the tzatziki on the side.

TO DRINK:
A Cabernet Sauvignon, like Honig from California

[Serves 4]

1 small English cucumber

Kosher salt

1 eggplant

3 tablespoons extra-virgin olive oil, plus more for the eggplant

2 tablespoons minced lemongrass, light part only (see Ming's Tip)

3 tablespoons minced garlic

1 cup Greek yogurt

8 mint leaves, cut into ⅛-inch strips

Juice and zest of 1 lemon

Freshly ground black pepper

8 loin lamb chops (about 3 pounds)

Ming's Tip:
To mince lemongrass, hit the light part with the side of a knife several times to break it down. The root end should pop off; if not, cut it away. Starting where the light part joins the darker, slice the light part lengthwise three or four times. Cut the light part crosswise and then mince. (You can use the darker part to make broth.)

TO DRINK:
A Dolcetto d'Alba, like Prunotto

asian spaghetti

[Serves 4]

1 pound spaghetti

Kosher salt

1 tablespoon extra-virgin olive oil, plus more for coating the pasta

2 large onions, cut into ¼-inch dice

2 tablespoons minced garlic

1 pound ground beef

1 pound ground pork

Freshly ground black pepper

One 32-ounce can roma tomatoes with their liquid

¼ cup naturally brewed soy sauce

2 tablespoons tomato paste

½ cup loosely packed Thai basil

Close your eyes, envision a spaghetti dish, and I bet you see tomato sauce. My attempt to transform the typical spaghetti-ragù pairing inspired this dish, which does include tomatoes but is otherwise exceptional. The key here is the addition of soy sauce, which adds *umami*, that intriguing "fifth taste" first explored by Japanese cooks. It also features Thai basil, one of my favorite herbs. This is much loved in my house and should be equally welcome in yours.

1. Fill a large bowl with water and add ice cubes. In a large pot, cook the pasta in abundant boiling salted water until al dente, about 11 minutes; drain, and add to the bowl. When the pasta is cold, drain, coat lightly with oil, and set aside.

2. Heat the pot over medium-high heat. Add the 1 tablespoon oil and when hot, add the onions and garlic. Sauté, stirring, until the onions are translucent, about 2 minutes. Add the beef and the pork, season with salt and pepper, and sauté, stirring to break up the meat, until lightly browned, about 5 minutes. Add the tomatoes with their liquid, the soy sauce, tomato paste, and basil and bring to a simmer. Adjust the seasoning, if necessary, and simmer until the liquid is reduced by a quarter, about 25 minutes. Add the reserved pasta to the pot and stir gently. Transfer to a platter or four individual plates and serve.

TO DRINK:
A pilsner lager, like Stella Artois

[Serves 4]

2 tablespoons grapeseed or canola oil

2 medium red onions, cut into ¼-inch dice

2 tablespoons minced garlic

1 tablespoon minced ginger

1 cup diced celery

1 tablespoon sambal or hot sauce of your choice

1¼ cups hoisin sauce

1 pound ground beef

1 pound ground pork

Juice of 2 limes

8 ounces roma tomatoes, fresh or canned, chopped

Kosher salt and freshly ground black pepper

4 hamburger buns

1 small head iceberg lettuce, shredded

—

Blue Ginger Multigrain Brown Rice Chips (see page 11) or other chips

Pickles, for serving

asian sloppy joes

Sloppy Joes were my mom's go-to dish when famished kids hung out at my house growing up. Of course, she gave it her own Asian twist, which I honor here: hoisin sauce for a touch of sweetness, ginger, pork, plus beef, garlic—of course—and a bit of sambal for heat. Adults are equally delighted by this easy, informal dish, which always looks invitingly, well, sloppy. Chips are the indispensible accompaniment here.

1. Heat a stockpot or other tall wide pot over high heat. Add the oil and swirl to coat the bottom. When the oil is hot, add the onions, garlic, ginger, celery and sambal. Sauté, stirring occasionally, until the onions are soft, about 2 minutes. Add the hoisin sauce and sauté 1 minute. Add the beef and pork and sauté, breaking up the meat, until just cooked through, about 6 minutes. Add the lime juice and tomatoes and season with salt and pepper. Reduce the heat to medium-low and simmer until the mixture has thickened enough to mound when ladled, 20 to 25 minutes.

2. Toast the buns and place a bottom half on each individual serving plate. Top generously with the meat mixture. Top with the lettuce and the bun tops. Serve with the chips and pickles.

Ming's Tip:

Make extra sloppy joe mixture, transfer to freezer bags, and freeze. It's great to have on hand for quick meal making.

black bean orecchiette with spicy pork and broccoli

TO DRINK:
A crisp Pinot Grigio, like Maso Canali from Italy.

I'm a huge orecchiette fan. The "tiny ears" are exceptionally chewy and really hold other ingredients, like the spicy pork in this recipe. The pork is complemented by fermented black beans, one of the deep Chinese flavorings; I think of them as soy sauce on steroids. This is a terrifically tasty dish and one, I've found, that kids really love. Serve it with big soup spoons and everyone's happy.

[Serves 4]

1 large head broccoli

Kosher salt

8 ounces orecchiette

2 tablespoons extra-virgin olive oil, plus more for drizzling

1 tablespoon minced garlic

2 tablespoons fermented black beans

1 tablespoon minced ginger

1 medium red onion, cut into 1/4-inch dice

1 cup dry white wine

1 pound ground pork

Freshly ground black pepper

1 teaspoon Korean chile pepper flakes or red pepper flakes, for garnish

1. Separate the broccoli into florets. Cut off their long stems and, using a chef's knife, square the stems so they resemble elongated blocks. Alternatively, peel the stems. Cut the stems into 1/4-inch pieces.

2. Fill a bowl large bowl with water and add ice cubes. Bring abundant salted water to a boil in a stockpot or other tall wide pot. Add the broccoli and blanch for 30 seconds, retrieve the broccoli with a large strainer, and transfer it in the strainer to the ice water. When the broccoli is cold, lift the strainer and drain the broccoli. Transfer the broccoli to a plate.

3. Return the water in the pot to a boil. Add more ice cubes to the bowl, if needed. Add the pasta to the pot and cook until al dente, about 10 minutes. Retrieve the pasta with the strainer and transfer the pasta to the bowl. Reserve 1/2 cup of the cooking liquid. When the pasta is cold, lift the strainer and drain the pasta.

4. Dry the pot and heat over medium heat. Add the olive oil to the pot and swirl to coat the bottom. When the oil is hot, add the garlic, black beans, ginger and onions and sauté, stirring, until the onions are soft, about 2 minutes. Add the wine, deglaze the pan, and simmer until the liquid is reduced by half, about 2 minutes. Season with salt and pepper. Add the pork and sauté, breaking up the meat, until just cooked through, 6 to 8 minutes.

5. Add the pasta and broccoli to the black-bean mixture and toss well. If the mixture seems dry, add the reserved cooking liquid. Season again with salt and pepper. Transfer to a large serving bowl or platter, garnish with the chile pepper flakes, drizzle with olive oil, and serve.

soba noodle carbonara

TO DRINK:
A light fruity Italian white wine, like Bastianich Friulano Colli Orientali de Friuli

Trying to make a good dish even better is a challenge I love. In the case of spaghetti carbonara, that much-enjoyed Italian specialty featuring pancetta, eggs and cheese, my first move was to substitute soba noodles for the spaghetti. Not only is buckwheat-based soba better for you than regular pasta, but it packs more flavor. Scallions, courtesy of the Asian pantry, add their own kick.

[Serves 4]

4 ounces soba noodles

Kosher salt

1 tablespoon grapeseed or canola oil

1/2 cup pancetta, cut into 1/4-inch dice

5 scallions, sliced thin, white and green parts separated

1 tablespoon minced garlic

1/2 cup heavy cream

About 1/4 cup freshly grated Parmigiano-Reggiano cheese, plus more for serving

3 tablespoons pasteurized liquid egg yolks

Freshly ground black pepper

1. Fill a large bowl with water and add ice cubes. In a stockpot or other tall pot, cook the soba in abundant boiling salted water until al dente, 3 to 4 minutes. Drain the pasta (reserving 1/3 cup of the cooking water) using a large strainer and transfer the strainer to the ice water. When the soba is cold, drain and set aside.

2. Heat the pot over medium-high heat. Add the oil and swirl to coat the bottom. When the oil is hot, add the pancetta. Sauté, stirring, until crisp, 6 to 8 minutes. Add the scallion whites and garlic and sauté for 1 minute. Add the cream, the reserved pasta water, and the cheese. Add the soba and toss to combine. Add the eggs and toss gently. Season with salt and pepper. Transfer immediately to four individual plates, garnish with the scallion greens, and serve with additional cheese.

Ming's Tip:

As the egg yolks remain uncooked in this, I call for pasteurized liquid yolks to ensure healthfulness.

TO DRINK:
A French Burgundy, like Louis Latour Santenay

[Serves 4]

2 tablespoons grapeseed or canola oil

1 pound small (51-60) shrimp, or rock shrimp, rinsed and dried

Kosher salt and freshly ground black pepper

3 tablespoons unsalted butter

2 tablespoons minced garlic

1 small onion, cut into 1/8-inch dice

2 cups koshikari or other sushi rice, or Arborio rice

1 cup dry white wine

5 to 6 cups fresh chicken stock or low-sodium canned chicken broth, hot

12 Thai basil leaves, cut into very fine strips

Juice of 1 lime

thai basil shrimp risotto

Some people think risotto is tricky to make. It's not. All you have to do is pay attention as you add ladlefuls of broth to the rice, so you can judge when the risotto is properly cooked. My Asian version features koshikari rice, a premium sushi rice that has a higher absorption threshold than that of other rices. Like its Italian cousin, Arborio, it can be cooked to a creamy-firm bite. Shrimp and Thai basil complete the dish.

1. Heat a large saucepan over medium-high heat. Add 1 tablespoon of the oil and swirl to coat the bottom. When the oil is hot, add the shrimp and sauté, stirring, until the shrimp are pink, about 1 minute. Season with salt and pepper. Transfer the shrimp to a plate and set aside.

2. Add the remaining tablespoon oil and 1 tablespoon of the butter. When the mixture is hot, add the garlic and onions and sauté until soft, 1 to 2 minutes. Add the rice and sauté, stirring, until the rice has become opaque, about 2 minutes. Add the wine, deglaze the pan, and simmer until the liquid has been absorbed by the rice, 2 to 3 minutes.

3. Ladle in the stock 1/2 cup at a time, allowing each addition to be absorbed by the rice before adding the next. Continue until the rice is al dente, about 10 minutes. Return the shrimp to the rice, add the basil, remaining 2 tablespoons butter, and lime juice, and stir. Taste and adjust the seasoning.

4. Transfer the risotto to four individual serving bowls and serve.

mom's famous vinegared shrimp

It's true: I have the world's best mom. She also makes the world's best food, including the traditional version of this shrimp dish, a beloved favorite of my childhood. It's based on a Chinese seasoning combination called 3-2-1, the proportion of sugar to soy sauce to vinegar in the recipe. Here, I use two vinegars—balsamic for its dark sweetness, rice vinegar for tartness—plus edamame, for texture. I also "francophile" the dish with butter, a touch that adds lusciousness. And there's Yukon Gold potatoes— another departure from Mom's dish, but delicious even so.

1. Preheat the oven to 375°F.

2. Wrap the potatoes in foil, prick them several times with a fork, and bake until cooked through, about 30 minutes.

3. Meanwhile, in a medium bowl combine the vinegars, sugar and soy sauce and stir until the sugar is dissolved. Set aside.

4. Heat a large sauté pan over high heat. Add 1 tablespoon of the oil. Add the shrimp and sauté, stirring, until the shrimp turn pink, about 1 minute. Transfer to a bowl and set aside.

5. Add the remaining oil to the pan and when hot, add the garlic, ginger, and shallots. Sauté until soft, about 2 minutes. Add the soy sauce mixture, deglaze the pan, and simmer until the mixture is reduced by half, 2 to 3 minutes. Add the edamame, tomato, and shrimp. Simmer until the shrimp are cooked through, 2 to 3 minutes. Whisk in the butter and season with salt and pepper.

6. Trim the ends from the potatoes and halve through the center. Divide the potatoes among four individual plates, top with the shrimp and sauce, and serve.

TO DRINK:
A white Burgundy, like Latour Puligny Montrachet or any other Montrachet

[Serves 4]

4 Yukon Gold potatoes, each about 3 inches in diameter

1/4 cup balsamic vinegar

1/4 cup naturally brewed rice vinegar

1 tablespoon sugar

1 tablespoon plus 1 teaspoon naturally brewed soy sauce

2 tablespoons grapeseed or canola oil

12 large (U-15) shrimp, peeled and deveined

2 tablespoons minced garlic

1 tablespoon minced ginger

2 medium shallots, sliced thin

1 cup shelled edamame

1 medium tomato, cut into 1/4-inch dice

4 tablespoons (1/2 stick) chilled unsalted butter

Kosher salt and freshly ground black pepper

TO DRINK:
A tropical fruit juice like pineapple or passion fruit or a New Zealand Sauvignon Blanc, like Brancott or Giesen

[Serves 4]

½ pound fresh or dried pappardelle

Kosher salt

2 tablespoons extra-virgin olive oil, plus more for coating the pasta

2 tablespoons minced lemongrass, white part only (see Ming's Tip, page 66)

4 shallots, sliced thin

1 tablespoon minced garlic

Freshly ground black pepper

12 large (U-15) shrimp, peeled and deveined

Zest and juice of 2 lemons

3 tablespoons unsalted butter

1 tablespoon thinly sliced chives, for garnish

lemongrass scampi with pappardelle

The Italian-American dish called "shrimp scampi" (a redundancy, as "scampi" is always a shrimp dish) features shrimp, garlic butter, lemon and parsley. We've had much success at Blue Ginger serving this version with lemongrass in addition to the citrus fruit, and pairing the shrimp with pappardelle, a pasta with lots of surface area for sauce-coating. This is a perfect starter or main dish, and it's easy to make, too.

1. Fill a large bowl with water and add ice. In a stockpot or other tall wide pot, cook the pappardelle in abundant boiling salted water until al dente, 1 to 2 minutes if fresh, 4 to 5 minutes if dried. Using a large strainer, transfer the pasta to the ice water, and when cold, drain and transfer to a medium bowl. Drizzle in enough oil to coat the pasta lightly, toss, and set aside. Reserve 1 cup of the cooking water.

2. Heat the stockpot over medium heat. Add the 2 tablespoons of oil and swirl to coat the bottom. When the oil is hot, add the lemongrass, shallots and garlic and sauté, stirring, for 1 minute. Season with salt and pepper. Add the shrimp and sauté until cooked through, 3 to 5 minutes. Add the lemon zest and juice, stir, and return the pasta to the pot. Toss to combine. Adjust the seasoning if necessary. If the mixture seems dry, add as much of the reserved pasta water, starting with 2 tablespoons, as needed. Add the butter, stir, and transfer to four individual serving plates. Garnish with the chives and serve.

seared curried butterfish with warm olive chutney

TO DRINK:
A Chenin Blanc, like Domaine Vigneau-Chevreau Cuvée Silex Vouvray from France

[Serves 4]

4 tablespoons Madras curry powder

1/2 cup rice flour, brown rice flower, or cornstarch

Four 6- to 8-ounce fillets butterfish, cod, or farm-raised Chilean sea bass

Kosher salt and freshly ground black pepper

4 tablespoons extra-virgin olive oil, plus more for drizzling

3 shallots, minced

1/2 cup mixed olives, pitted and minced

1 large tomato, cut into 1/4-inch dice

Juice of 1 orange

2 tablespoons chopped cilantro

Butterfish, also known as black cod or sablefish, is delicious, succulent seafood. A curry rub not only gives the fish great flavor, but helps to color it richly. I devised this dish after tasting South African cooking, which melds native and European ingredients intriguingly—my inspiration for putting olives in the sprightly chutney accompaniment. Curry and olives is one of those great combos that people should be more aware of, and definitely will be when they try this.

1. On a large platter, combine the curry powder and rice flour and mix well. Season the fish with salt and pepper and dredge it on both sides in the flour mixture.

2. Heat a large heavy skillet that can be brought to the table over medium-high heat. When the pan is very hot, add 2 tablespoons of the oil and swirl to coat the bottom. When the oil is hot, add the fish. Sauté the fish, turning once, until a paring knife pierces it easily, about 8 minutes. Remove the fish and set aside.

3. Add the remaining 2 tablespoons olive oil, swirl, and when hot, add the shallots, olives, tomato and orange juice. Heat through, about 2 minutes. Add the cilantro and stir to combine.

4. Return the fish to the pan, drizzle with oil, and serve.

Ming's Tip:

To prevent the fish from sticking to the pan, make sure the pan is very hot before adding oil. The oil should appear to shimmer or dance before adding the fish. If the fish sticks anyway, don't try to dislodge it. Allow the fish to crust and it will release by itself.

soba-noodle shrimp pancakes

This is my take on Japanese *okonomiyaki*, pancakes with savory toppings. In some okonomiyaki restaurants, customers cook their own pancakes on an iron griddle set in the table. My kitchen-cooked version uses soba noodles to make free-form pancake "sandwiches," which are filled with a delicious, shrimp-based purée. These are fun to do, and they make an impressive showing for guests.

1. Fill a large bowl with water and add ice cubes. In a large pot, cook the noodles in abundant boiling salted water until al dente, about 5 minutes. Using a large strainer, drain and transfer the noodles to the ice water. When the noodles are cold, drain and set aside.

2. Heat the pot over medium heat. Add the pancetta and sauté until crisp, 8 to 10 minutes. Drain the pancetta on a paper towel and set aside.

3. In a small bowl, combine the mayonnaise, Worcestershire sauce and the larger quantity of scallion greens. Season with salt and pepper. Set aside.

4. Add the eggs and shrimp to a food processor and pulse until the mixture is roughly puréed. Transfer the mixture to a medium bowl, add the parsley, pancetta and scallion whites, and fold to combine.

5. To make the pancakes, place ¼-cup portions of the noodles on a work surface. Flatten to make about 16 pancakes about 3 inches in diameter. Top each with 1 heaping tablespoon of the shrimp purée, top with the remaining noodles, and flatten to make ½-inch-thick pancakes.

6. Add the oil to a nonstick sauté pan and heat over medium-high heat. Using a spatula, and working in batches if necessary, add the pancakes and sauté, turning once, until crispy, 4 to 5 minutes.

7. Place streaks of the mayonnaise mixture on serving plates, top with the pancakes, garnish with the remaining scallion greens, and serve.

TO DRINK:
A Marsanne, like Treana Mer Soleil Vineyard Viognier–Marsanne from California

[Serves 4]

8 ounces soba noodles

Kosher salt

½ cup pancetta, cut into ½-inch dice

½ cup mayonnaise

1 tablespoon organic Worcestershire sauce

1 bunch scallions, sliced thin, white and green parts separated, 1 tablespoon of the greens reserved for garnish

Freshly ground black pepper

2 large eggs

1 pound small (51-60) shrimp, rinsed and drained

¼ cup chopped parsley

2 tablespoons grapeseed or canola oil, plus more, if needed

potato-crusted halibut
with shaved fennel salad

TO DRINK:
A chilled sake like TY KU Black

[Serves 4]

Juice of 2 limes

6 tablespoons grapeseed or canola oil

2 tablespoons chopped chives

3 fennel bulbs, cored and sliced very thin
(see Ming's Tip, page 45)

Kosher salt and freshly ground black pepper

2 eggs

1 cup rice flour or all-purpose flour

1 cup large potato flakes (dehydrated
mashed-potato flakes)

1 pound skinless halibut, cut into four
4-ounce fillets

This is one of my favorite springtime-summertime dishes. Halibut, a lean, mild-tasting fish, is coated with rice flour and dehydrated potato flakes— a terrific, more delicate alternative to bread crumbs—sautéed, and served with a lime-dressed fennel salad. You'll be amazed at the tasty elegance of this dish, which is really fun to do, too.

1. To make the salad, combine the lime juice, 4 tablespoons of the oil, and the chives in a large bowl and whisk to blend. Just before cooking the fish, add the fennel, stir, season with salt and pepper, and let macerate while the fish cooks.

2. Beat the eggs lightly in a shallow bowl. Spread the flour on a medium plate and the potato flakes on a second. Season the fish with salt and pepper on both sides. One by one, coat the fish fillets lightly with the flour, dip them into the egg, and then coat with the potato flakes.

3. Heat a large sauté pan over medium heat. Add the remaining 2 tablespoons oil and swirl to coat the bottom. When the oil is hot, add the fish and sauté, turning once, until the fish is golden brown and just cooked through, about 6 minutes. Divide the salad among four individual serving plates, top with the fish, and serve.

vegetarian paella

To me, paella is the best family-style dish ever. The traditional version is, however, something of a production, involving multiple kinds of seafood plus, usually, chicken and sausage. My take uses vegetables only, including sweet potato and edamame, and sushi rice, which absorbs more of the flavorful braising liquid than other types. The dish is rich and satisfying, so you never miss the seafood.

1. Heat a large paella pan or large skillet over medium-high heat. Add the oil and swirl to coat the bottom. When the oil is hot, add the onions, lemongrass, garlic and ginger and sauté, stirring, until soft, about 2 minutes. Season with salt and pepper.

2. Add the rice and paprika and sauté, stirring, until the rice is coated with oil. Add the wine, deglaze the pan, and simmer until the liquid is reduced by three quarters, about 2 minutes. Add the stock and parsley, stir, and add the potato and edamame. Adjust the seasoning, if necessary. Reduce the heat to low and simmer gently, covered, until the rice is cooked, 25 to 30 minutes. Allow to rest for 5 minutes, and serve from the pan.

TO DRINK:
A Spanish rosé, like Muga Rioja

[Serves 4]

2 tablespoons extra-virgin olive oil

1 large onion, minced

4 stalks lemongrass, white part only, minced (see Ming's Tip, page 66)

2 tablespoons minced garlic

1 tablespoon minced ginger

Kosher salt and freshly ground black pepper

2 cups sushi rice

1 tablespoon paprika

1 cup dry white wine

4 cups vegetable stock

1/2 bunch parsley, roughly chopped

1 large sweet potato, peeled, cut into 1/2-inch dice

1 cup shelled edamame

asian ratatouille with whole-wheat couscous

If you doubt that a meatless dish can be just as satisfying as one that isn't, you must try this. I first made ratatouille in Paris—a bit far from its terroir, but a revelation to me nonetheless. Prepared with super-flavorful fermented black beans and other Asian ingredients, and served with whole-wheat couscous, ratatouille becomes a really mighty dish, and one that's surprisingly light.

1. Heat a medium sauté pan over high heat. Add 2 tablespoons of the oil and when hot, add the onions and eggplant. Season with salt and pepper and sauté, stirring, until the vegetables are soft, about 3 minutes. Add the garlic and beans and sauté for 1 minute. Add the peppers and zucchini and sauté until slightly softened, about 3 minutes, then add the tomato and thyme. Stir and adjust the seasoning, if necessary. Reduce the heat to low and cook until soft, 10 to 12 minutes. Check the seasoning one more time.

2. Meanwhile, make the couscous. In a medium saucepan, bring 3 cups water to a boil. Add the couscous, stir, cover, and simmer until the water is absorbed, about 2 minutes. Fluff with a fork, turn off the heat, cover, and allow to stand for 5 minutes. Fluff again and stir in the basil strips. Season with salt and pepper.

3. Fill a small ring mold, an emptied and thoroughly washed tuna can, or a small rice bowl with the couscous and invert onto an individual serving plate. Repeat with three more serving plates. Alternatively, transfer the couscous to four pasta bowls. Top the couscous with the ratatouille, drizzle with the oil, garnish with the basil sprigs, and serve.

TO DRINK:
A sparkling wine from the Loire Valley, like Charles de Fère Réserve Blanc de Blancs Brut

[Serves 4]

4 tablespoons extra-virgin olive oil, plus more for drizzling

1 small red onion, cut into 1/4-inch dice

2 Japanese eggplants, or 1 small regular eggplant, unpeeled, cut into 1/2-inch dice

Kosher salt and freshly ground black pepper

2 tablespoons minced garlic

2 tablespoons fermented black beans

2 red bell peppers, cut into 1/2-inch dice

2 medium zucchini, cut into 1/2-inch dice

1 cup tomato, preferably heirloom, cut into 1/2-inch dice

2 tablespoons minced fresh thyme

2 cups instant whole-wheat couscous

8 Thai basil leaves, cut into thin strips, plus sprigs for garnish

2 tablespoons wheat-free tamari sauce

TO DRINK:
A Dolcetto D'Alba, like Bruno
Giacosa

[Serves 4]

3 tablespoons extra-virgin olive oil

1 tablespoon minced garlic

4 cups wild mushrooms, such as oyster,
chanterelles, or lobster, or shiitakes,
individually or in combination, torn apart or
sliced thin, depending on size and shape

Kosher salt and freshly ground black pepper

2 tablespoons unsalted butter

1 medium onion, minced

2 cups milk

4 cups fresh chicken stock or low-sodium
canned chicken broth

1½ cups instant polenta

½ cup shaved or grated Parmigiano-
Reggiano cheese

½ cup lightly packed Thai basil leaves,
or regular basil

Zest of 1 lemon and juice of ½ lemon

1 teaspoon pink peppercorns, finger-crushed

wild mushroom polenta with thai basil salad

Mushrooms are the vegetarian meat. Their chewy texture and deep satisfying flavor—mushrooms are rich in *umami*—make this dish super-tasty. Next to rice, polenta is my favorite starch; it's particularly great when combined with mushrooms and paired with a sprightly basil salad. This all cooks very fast, too, so it's a great dish to make when time is short.

1. Heat a medium saucepan over medium heat. Add 2 tablespoons of the oil and swirl to coat the bottom. When the oil is hot, add the garlic and sauté, stirring, until soft, about 1 minute. Add the mushrooms and sauté until lightly cooked, 3 to 4 minutes. Season with salt and pepper. Transfer the mixture to a plate and set aside.

2. Add 1 tablespoon of the butter and the remaining tablespoon of oil to the pan. When the butter has melted, add the onions and sauté, stirring, until softened, about 3 minutes. Season with salt and pepper. Add the milk and stock and bring to a simmer. Whisking the liquid, add the polenta in a fine steady stream, reduce the heat to low, and cook, whisking from time to time, until creamy and smooth, 3 to 4 minutes. Adjust the seasoning, if necessary. Just before serving, whisk in the remaining tablespoon butter, the cheese and the mushrooms.

3. In a small bowl, combine the basil and the lemon zest and juice. Season with salt and pepper and toss lightly. Transfer the polenta to four individual bowls, top with the basil salad, sprinkle with the pink peppercorns, and serve.

Ming's Tip:

When shopping, buy the freshest mushrooms available, no matter the type. Always substitute when a specific ingredient doesn't measure up to a fresher one that can be used interchangeably.

sweet potato ravioli with brown thai-basil butter

My good friend Mario Batali of Manhattan's award-winning Babbo restaurant inspired this dish. His delicious version pairs sweet potato ravioli with brown butter and sage; mine uses convenient wonton wrappers to make the ravioli and features Thai basil. A touch of honey and five-spice powder in the ravioli filling tilts my dish farther toward the East. And speaking of the East, the Chinese did invent pasta, though if you cook as wonderfully as Mario, that's way beside the point.

1. Preheat the oven to 375°F. Wrap the potatoes in foil, prick several times with a fork, and bake until soft, about 45 minutes.

2. Scoop the potato meat into a medium bowl. Add the five-spice powder, the larger quantity of chives and the honey. Season with salt and pepper.

3. When the filling has cooled, make the ravioli: Center 1 basil leaf on 1 wonton wrapper, top with 1 tablespoon of the filling, and top with a second basil leaf. Brush the edges of the wrapper with the egg mixture, top with a second wrapper, and seal by pressing outward along the edges with a finger. Repeat to make about 20 ravioli.

4. Line a large plate with paper towels. Add 2 tablespoons of the butter to a large sauté pan and heat over medium heat. When hot, add half the ravioli and sauté until brown and crisp, turning once, about 4 minutes. Transfer the ravioli to the plate. Using 2 more tablespoons butter, sauté the remaining ravioli and transfer to the plate. Divide the ravioli among four individual serving plates.

5. Add the remaining 4 tablespoons butter to the pan and cook until the butter has browned lightly, 2 to 3 minutes. Standing back to avoid any splatters, add the remaining basil from the 1/4 cup, and the vinegar and mix.

6. Drizzle the sauce over the ravioli, garnish with chives, and serve.

TO DRINK:
A Light Oregon Pinot Noir,
like Andrew Rich

[Serves 4 as an entrée]

2 large sweet potatoes

1 teaspoon five-spice powder

1 bunch chives, sliced fine, 1 tablespoon reserved for garnish

2 tablespoons honey

Kosher salt and freshly ground black pepper

1/4 cup packed Thai basil leaves

One 12-ounce package square wonton wrappers

1 large egg mixed with 2 tablespoons water

8 tablespoons (1 stick) unsalted butter

1/4 cup balsamic vinegar

4

Think roasting and you probably picture a turkey served with "fixings" you've prepared separately. But there's an easier way. Following my one-pot approach, a "main" item like pork, lamb, or chicken is cooked with other ingredients to create a dish that's complete in itself. Dishes such as Ginger Chicken Thighs with Parsnips and Chile Pork Fillets with Garlic Brussels Sprouts showcase this approach, which recasts the roasting pan as a kind of casserole.

One-pot roasting has other advantages. Once your dish is in the oven and you've set your timer, you can walk away from the stove without needing to return until the dish is done. Kids ready to eat before the adults, or someone's detained? Serve some of your roast now and the rest will still be fine later. Roasting can be perfect for entertaining, too. A dish like Miso-Marinated Lamb with Carrots and Potatoes can be started before guests arrive, then served with little last-minute attention. People think of roasting as "big deal," but with my one-pot approach it's "everyday."

ROAST

orange-yuzu glazed chicken with wild rice salad

Yuzu juice, which comes from the Japanese citrus fruit, has a wonderfully intriguing flavor. It tastes like lemongrass and lime leaf combined, and it makes the chicken in this recipe exotically delicious. Yuzu is also used in the dressing for the wild rice accompaniment. I love wild rice, a grain some people think of as old-fashioned but that I call timeless. This makes a great company or weekend family dish.

1. To make the glaze, combine the orange juice, yuzu juice, and honey in a small bowl. Season with salt and pepper. Remove ¼ cup of the mixture to a second small bowl and set both bowls aside.

2. Fill a large bowl with water and add ice. Cook the beans in abundant boiling water until tender-crisp, 2 to 3 minutes for haricots verts, 4 to 5 minutes for regular beans. Using a large strainer, transfer the beans to the ice water. When cold, drain the beans. If using regular beans, cut them into 1-inch lengths. Set the beans aside.

3. Preheat the oven to 375°F. Season the chicken well with salt and pepper.

4. Heat a large, heavy skillet over high heat. Add the oil and swirl to coat the bottom. When the oil is hot, add the chicken and brown, turning once, 8 to 10 minutes. Transfer to a platter and pour out all but 1 tablespoon of the fat. Reduce the heat to medium and add the onions. Season with salt and pepper and sauté, stirring, until softened, 5 to 7 minutes.

5. Return the chicken to the pan and brush with the glaze. Transfer to the oven, bake for 10 minutes, and brush again with the glaze. Return the pan to the oven and bake until the chicken is done, 20 to 25 minutes in all. Transfer the onions to a large bowl.

6. Meanwhile, in a small bowl, blend the orange zest, mustard, the reserved ¼ cup of brushing syrup and the yogurt.

7. Add the rice and beans to the bowl with the onions. Add all but 2 tablespoons of the mustard-yogurt mixture and toss lightly. Season with salt and pepper.

8. Carve the chicken. Transfer the rice salad to four individual plates and add a dollop of the remaining mustard-yogurt mixture to one side.

TO DRINK:
A Crisp Loire Valley wine, New Zealand Sauvignon Blanc, or Prosecco like Cantina Produttori de Valdobbiadene Val d'Oca

[Serves 4]

2 tablespoons orange juice and grated zest of ½ orange

2 tablespoons yuzu juice or naturally brewed ponzu

½ cup honey

Kosher salt and freshly ground black pepper

½ pound haricots verts, or regular string beans, stem-ends trimmed

One 6-pound chicken, split, washed, and patted dry

2 tablespoons grapeseed or canola oil

2 red onions, cut into 1-inch slices

1 tablespoon Dijon mustard

½ cup Greek yogurt

2 cups cooked wild rice (see page 12); save extra rice for another use

Ming's Tip:
You can make the glaze ahead of time and store it in a lidded plastic container in the fridge.

TO DRINK:
A Shiraz or Syrah, like Radio-Coteau
Timbervine from California

ginger chicken thighs with parsnips

[Serves 4]

2 pounds chicken thighs

Kosher salt and freshly ground black pepper

3 tablespoons grapeseed or canola oil

2 large onions, cut into 1-inch dice

2 tablespoons minced ginger

3 large parsnips, peeled and roll-cut into 1-inch lengths (see page 13), or cut conventionally

4 celery stalks, roll-cut into 1-inch lengths (see page 13), or cut conventionally

5 sprigs fresh thyme

Chicken thighs are my favorite part of the bird. They've got just the right meat-to-skin ratios and they really shine in this quick, gingery bake that's great for post-work cooking. This dish also features parsnips, which I think of as white carrots. They're as sweet as carrots but have more character.

1. Preheat the oven to 450°F.

2. Season the thighs with the salt and pepper. Heat a large heavy roasting pan or heavy skillet over medium-high heat. Add 2 tablespoons of the oil and swirl to coat the bottom. When the oil is hot, add the thighs skin side down. Brown, turning once, about 10 minutes. Transfer the thighs to a platter and set aside.

3. Add the remaining oil to the pan, swirl, and heat. When the oil is hot, add the onions, ginger, parsnips, celery and thyme. Season with salt and pepper and sauté the vegetables, stirring, until softened, about 6 minutes. Top with the thighs, skin side up, and bake uncovered until the chicken and vegetables are done, 30 to 40 minutes. Transfer to a platter or four individual serving plates and serve.

mushroom chicken fricassee with edamame

TO DRINK:
An Oregon Pinot Noir, like Argyle Reserve

Everyone loves homey chicken fricassee—and my version is super-easy, as well as delicious. You brown the chicken—legs plus thighs, the most flavorful parts of the bird—add mushrooms and aromatics, liquid and edamame, and bake. In about forty minutes you have a great, savory meal. This is a terrific dish for after-work cooking, of course, but I find myself making it even if I have spare time.

1. Preheat the oven to 400°F. Season the chicken with salt and pepper.

2. Heat a large roasting pan or large heavy skillet over medium-high heat. Add the oil and swirl to coat the bottom. When the oil is hot, add the chicken and sauté, turning once, until brown, about 10 minutes. Transfer to a plate and set aside.

3. Drain the pan of all but 1 tablespoon of the fat. Add the onions, garlic and mushrooms and sauté until lightly brown, 2 to 3 minutes, and season with salt and pepper. Add the tarragon, tomatoes with their liquid, and edamame. Mix well and adjust the seasoning, if necessary. Top with the chicken, transfer to the oven, and bake until the chicken is cooked through, 20 to 25 minutes. Transfer to a platter and serve.

[Serves 4]

2 pounds unskinned bone-in chicken legs with thighs

Salt and freshly ground black pepper

2 tablespoons grapeseed or canola oil

1 large red onion, halved and sliced 1/4 inch thick

1 tablespoon minced garlic

1 pound mushrooms, sliced 1/4 inch thick

2 tablespoons minced fresh tarragon

2 cups canned whole roma tomatoes, roughly chopped, with the juice from measuring

1 cup shelled edamame

TO DRINK:
A Pinot Noir, like any Ken Wright
from Oregon or Hill of Content
from Australia

[Serves 4]

8 duck legs (legs plus thighs)

Kosher salt and freshly ground black pepper

2 tablespoons grapeseed or canola oil

2 slices thick-cut bacon

2 medium onions, sliced thick

Six 1/2-inch-thick slices peeled ginger, cut
lengthwise from a 2- to 4-inch piece

1 serrano chile, halved lengthwise

3 medium oranges, quartered

1 cup carrot nubs

4 celery stalks, cut into 1/2-inch lengths

2 cups shelled edamame

1/2 cup Grand Marnier or other orange
liqueur

1/4 cup naturally brewed soy sauce

2 cups fresh chicken stock or low-sodium
canned chicken broth

ginger-orange duck "cassoulet"

I love duck legs, sold as leg-thigh combos. They're not only incredibly tasty but are easier to handle than a whole duck, which often needs to be disjointed before cooking. Like traditional cassoulet, this is a great one-pot meal. However, it uses edamame instead of the customary heavier beans, and it features the bright freshness of orange. Serve this with good bread.

1. Preheat the oven to 350°F.

2. Season the duck legs with salt and pepper. Heat a large ovenproof casserole over medium heat, add the oil, and swirl to coat the bottom. When the oil is hot, and working in batches if necessary, add the duck legs skin side down. Brown, turning once, about 20 minutes. If the legs haven't rendered most of their fat, cook a little longer. Transfer the legs to a plate and pour off all the fat (reserve the fat for future use).

3. Add the bacon, onions, ginger and chile. Season with salt and pepper and sauté until the vegetables have softened slightly, about 2 minutes. Add the oranges, carrots, celery and edamame and deglaze with the Grand Marnier. Add the soy sauce and stock and adjust the seasoning if necessary. Return the duck legs to the casserole, cover, and bake until a paring knife passes easily through the duck, about 2 hours. Serve from the casserole or transfer to a large shallow bowl and serve.

TO DRINK:
A Pinot Noir, like Penner Ash
from Oregon

[Serves 4]

1½ pounds uncooked chicken sausage
(see page 11)

1½ cups coarsely ground coriander seed
(see Ming's Tip)

2 tablespoons grapeseed or canola oil

2 medium onions, cut into 1-inch dice

3 fennel bulbs, halved, cored, and sliced
¼-inch thick

3 celery stalks, cut into 1-inch dice

Kosher salt and freshly ground black pepper

2 cups jasmine rice, or 1 cup jasmine and
1 cup brown rice

4 cups fresh chicken stock or low-sodium
canned chicken broth

Ming's Tip:

Use a heavy pan and cutting board
to crush the coriander seed.

If you make this following the
jasmine plus brown rice option,
the brown rice will cook up a bit
chewier than the jasmine, providing
textural interest.

chicken sausage
with fennel rice pilaf

As a pork-sausage lover, I used to scoff at chicken sausage. Now I know better. Buy a good chicken-sausage brand, and you get spicy, unctuous eating equal to that of the pork kind. In this dish, chicken sausage is made into coriander-scented meatballs that are baked with fennel and jasmine or brown rice—or, my preference, a half-half combination. This is delicious eating and is a particularly great dish for easy entertaining.

1. Preheat the oven to 375°F. Remove the sausage meat from the casings and roll into ½-inch balls.

2. Place the coriander in a large shallow plate, add the sausage balls, and turn to coat with the coriander. Heat an ovenproof casserole or large heavy skillet over high heat, add the oil, and swirl to coat the bottom. When the oil is hot, add the sausage balls and sauté on all sides until brown, about 6 minutes. Transfer the balls to a plate and set aside.

3. Reduce the heat to medium. Add the onions, fennel and celery to the pan and season with salt and pepper. Sauté, stirring, until browned, about 8 minutes. Add the rice, stir to combine, and add the sausage balls. Add the stock and bring to a simmer. Cover, transfer the pan to the oven, and bake until the rice is cooked, about 40 minutes. Remove the pan from the oven and let it stand, covered, for 15 minutes. Serve from the pan or transfer the mixture to a platter and serve.

jerk chicken with mango

Several theories exist about how jerk chicken got its name. The one I was first told, and that I'll stick with, links the name with the practice of jerking—poking—holes in the meat for spice-filling before the bird is cooked. It's a wonderful dish no matter its name's derivation, especially when paired with mangoes that have been cooked until caramelized and chewy. Jerk chicken is traditionally served with French fries. All I can say is, knock yourself out!

1. Make the marinade a day in advance: Using a mortar and pestle, or in a small food processor, combine the garlic, ginger, thyme, five-spice powder, black pepper, sambal, orange zest, 1 tablespoon of the sugar, and the salt and purée. Add the orange juice and oil and combine.

2. Coat the chicken inside and out with the jerk paste and marinate, covered and refrigerated, overnight.

3. Preheat the oven to 475°F. In a small bowl combine the mangoes, remaining sugar and the lime juice. Toss to coat the mangoes.

4. Transfer the chicken to a roasting pan and roast, rotating the pan once, until the chicken has browned, 25 to 35 minutes. Reduce the oven to 325°F, tent lightly with foil, and continue to roast the chicken until done, about 1 hour more. About 20 minutes before the chicken is done, add the mangoes to the pan, and cook until caramelized.

5. Transfer the chicken to a cutting board and allow to rest 10 minutes. Transfer the chicken to a platter, surround with the mangoes, carve at the table, and serve.

TO DRINK:
Dark and Stormy cocktails

[Serves 4]

6 garlic cloves

2 tablespoons minced ginger

2 tablespoons minced fresh thyme

2 tablespoons five-spice powder

1 tablespoon freshly ground black pepper

2 tablespoons sambal, or 1 small habernero or scotch bonnet chile, minced

Zest and juice of 1 large orange

2 tablespoons dark brown sugar

–

1 tablespoon kosher salt

1/4 cup grapeseed or canola oil

One 5- to 6-pound chicken

2 mangoes, peeled and cut into wedges

Juice of 1 lime

TO DRINK:
An unoaked Chardonnay, like
Morgan Metallico from California
or Truro from Massachusetts

[Serves 4]

2 tablespoons grapeseed or canola oil

8 chicken thighs with skin

Kosher salt and freshly ground black pepper

2 tablespoons minced garlic

2 bunches scallions, sliced thin

2 cups jasmine rice

¼ cup hoisin sauce

1 cup dry red wine

1 cup fresh cranberries

3 cups fresh chicken stock or low-sodium canned chicken broth

cranberry-hoisin chicken 'n' rice

I've always loved the chicken-with-rice dishes of Singapore, which are riffs on poached chicken served on savory rice. My one-pot version really shouts chicken flavor, as the rice is sautéed in chicken fat before it's baked. I love tasty chicken fat, but if you're concerned about its healthfulness, remove most of it from the casserole before adding the aromatics. Tart cranberries balance the richness of the dish while taming the sweetness of the hoisin. This is a perfect dish for entertaining.

1. Preheat the oven to 375°F.

2. Choose a large ovenproof casserole with a tight-fitting lid and place the casserole over medium-high heat. Add the oil and swirl to coat the bottom. When the oil is hot, add the chicken, in batches if necessary. Season with salt and pepper and sauté on all sides until lightly colored, about 8 minutes. Transfer to a plate and set aside.

3. Add the garlic and scallions to the casserole and sauté, stirring, for 1 minute. Add the rice and sauté, stirring, for 1 minute. Add the hoisin sauce and sauté for 30 seconds. Add the wine, deglaze, and simmer until the liquid is reduced by three quarters, about 2 minutes. Add the cranberries and stock and season with salt and pepper. Return the chicken to the casserole and bring to a simmer.

4. Cover the pot, transfer to the oven, and cook until the chicken is tender and the rice is cooked, 20 to 30 minutes. Remove from the oven and allow to rest for 10 minutes. Bring the pan to the table and serve.

moroccan spiced lamb shoulder with bell pepper COUSCOUS

TO DRINK:
A Bordeaux, like Calon-Ségur or Lynch Bages

Visiting Morocco I became aware of the great job done there with "lesser" meat cuts, like lamb shoulder. The shoulder has great flavor and good fat content—and when marinated overnight, it cooks up tasty as well as tender. The secret is a full-flavored marinade, which it gets here. The lamb is also roasted on a bed of onions, which pick up the savoriness of the lamb fat and juice. Served with couscous, the traditional Moroccan accompaniment, this is a feast.

[Serves 4]

2 tablespoons minced fresh thyme

4 tablespoons minced garlic

2 tablespoons coarsely ground coriander seed

2 tablespoons coarsely ground black pepper

2 tablespoons coarsely ground cumin seed

2 tablespoons coarsely ground fennel seed

1 tablespoon ground cinnamon

1 tablespoon paprika

2 tablespoons honey

1 tablespoon ancho chile powder

1 tablespoon kosher salt, plus more for seasoning

1 cup extra-virgin olive oil, 2 tablespoons reserved

One 5- to 6-pound boned lamb shoulder, spread flat

3 large onions, cut lengthwise 1/4 inch thick

Freshly ground black pepper

2 cups couscous

3 red bell peppers, cut into 1/4-inch dice

1. In a medium bowl, combine the thyme, garlic, coriander, coarsely ground black pepper, cumin, fennel, cinnamon, paprika, honey, chile powder and 1 tablespoon salt. Add the cup of olive oil and stir to blend. Transfer 1/2 cup of the mixture to a serving bowl and refrigerate, covered. Coat both sides of the lamb with the remaining mixture and transfer to a large resealable plastic bag. Marinate, refrigerated, for at least 2 hours or overnight.

2. Preheat the oven to 500°F. Place the onions on a large sheet tray or in a roasting pan and season with salt and pepper. Top with the lamb, transfer any remaining marinade to a bowl, and roast the lamb until brown, about 15 minutes.

3. Reduce the heat to 375°F. Turn the lamb, brush on the remaining marinade, and roast until the lamb is 120°F for medium-rare, 130°F for medium, or 140°F for medium-well, 20 to 25 minutes. Transfer the onions to a medium bowl and the lamb to a cutting board, and allow the lamb to rest for 10 minutes.

4. Meanwhile, make the couscous: Bring 3 cups of salted water to a boil in a medium saucepan. Add the couscous, drizzle with the 2 tablespoons of oil, stir, remove from the heat, and cover. Let stand until the couscous has absorbed the water, 4 to 5 minutes. Fluff with a fork. Add the bell peppers and stir lightly to blend.

5. Slice the lamb thin on the bias. Serve with the couscous, onions and reserved marinade.

wine and black-bean pot roast with smashed potatoes

TO DRINK:
A big red wine from Chile, like Montes Purple Angel Carmenere

[Serves 4]

8 medium Yukon Gold potatoes

One 8- to 10-pound piece top round or brisket

Kosher salt and freshly ground black pepper

2 tablespoons grapeseed or canola oil

2 tablespoons minced fermented black beans

2 tablespoons minced garlic

1 tablespoon minced ginger

1 bunch scallions, sliced thin

1 bottle red wine

1 quart fresh chicken stock or low-sodium canned chicken broth

1-pound bag carrot nubs

2 sprigs fresh rosemary

¼ cup naturally brewed soy sauce

Ming's Tip:
You can use a large slow-cooker to make this. Once everything is added to the pot, count on about 6 hours for the dish to be done.

Pot roast is a grandmotherly dish with many variations, depending, usually, on where one's grandmother—or great-grandmother—came from. China is my answer, so my version uses fermented black beans for deep, enticing flavor. Technically, this is a shallow braise, but I hope you'll allow me a little culinary license because the beef is actually baked, very slowly, to doneness. Rough-textured smashed potatoes—some people call them mashed "country-style"—complete the meal.

1. Preheat the oven to 250°F. Wrap the potatoes in foil and pierce several times with a fork. Set aside.

2. Season the beef generously with salt and pepper. Heat a large casserole or heavy roasting pan over medium-high heat. Add the oil and swirl to coat the bottom. When the oil is hot, add the beef and sauté on all sides until brown, about 15 minutes. Transfer the beef to a plate and set aside.

3. Pour off all but 2 tablespoons of fat from the pan. Add the beans, garlic, ginger, and scallions and sauté until softened, about 2 minutes. Add the wine, deglaze the pan, and reduce the liquid by half, 5 to 6 minutes. Add the stock, carrots, rosemary and soy sauce, stir, and season with salt and pepper. Cover the casserole, or if using a roasting pan, cover tightly with foil. Transfer to the oven and cook until a fork passes easily through the meat, about 4 hours. After 2½ hours of cooking, place the potatoes in the oven.

4. Remove the casserole and potatoes and allow the meat to stand in its liquid, covered, for 20 minutes. Transfer the roast to a carving board and allow to rest for 5 minutes. Meanwhile, transfer the casserole with the braising liquid to a burner and reduce the liquid over high heat for about 5 minutes.

5. Slice half the roast ⅛ inch thick and transfer the slices plus the remaining half to the casserole. Spoon the potatoes into a medium bowl and mash roughly. Bring the casserole and potatoes to the table, and serve.

miso-marinated lamb racks with carrots and potatoes

When you're cooking for a special occasion and can blow a little cash to make something really great, lamb racks are the thing. I prefer New Zealand racks for their smaller eyes and "gamier" taste, but, truthfully, I've never met a lamb rack I didn't like. In this dish racks are marinated in a miso-sake mixture that gives them enticing taste, then roasted with Yukon Gold potatoes and carrots. This is "one-pot" cooking that's easy as well as elegant.

1. In a large bowl, combine the miso, shallots, wasabi, sugar and sake and stir to blend. Whisk in the oil and blend. Set aside ¼ cup of the marinade.

2. Add the lamb racks to the bowl, turn to coat them, cover, and marinate, refrigerated, 2 to 4 hours.

3. Preheat the oven to 400°F. Choose a heavy roasting pan or heavy ovenproof skillet large enough to hold the racks and heat in the oven until very hot, about 10 minutes. Meanwhile, in a medium bowl combine the potatoes, carrots, scallion whites and reserved marinade. Toss and season with salt and pepper.

4. Open the oven, pull out the oven rack with the pan, and add the potato mixture. The mixture will sizzle. Top with the lamb racks and roast until a meat thermometer inserted in the thickest part of the meat registers 115° to 118°F for medium-rare, 15 to 20 minutes. (Or use a knife to determine doneness, see Ming's Tip.) Remove the racks and let them rest for 10 minutes. Transfer the potato mixture to a platter, top with the racks, garnish with the scallion greens, and serve.

TO DRINK:
A Bordeaux blend, like Cain Five from California

[Serves 4]

½ cup shiro miso

2 large shallots, minced

1 tablespoon rehydrated wasabi powder or wasabi paste

1 tablespoon sugar

½ cup sake

½ cup grapeseed or canola oil

2 lamb racks, about 2 pounds each

2 large Yukon Gold potatoes, unpeeled, washed and cut into 1-inch dice

1-pound bag peeled carrot nubs

1 cup scallions, sliced fine, white and green parts separated

Kosher salt and freshly ground black pepper

Ming's Tip:

To test the racks for doneness, insert a paring knife into the thickest part of the meat, remove it, and touch its tip to your lower lip. If the knife is cool, the meat is rare; if not quite warm, medium-rare; if warm, medium; if hot, medium-well.

chile pork fillets with garlic brussels sprouts

TO DRINK:
A big buttery California Central Coast Chardonnay, like Peter Michael

[Serves 4]

⅓ cup kosher salt, for brining, plus more for seasoning

¼ cup sugar

Four 8-ounce pork fillets cut from the loin

3 tablespoons ancho chile powder, or other chile powder

2 tablespoons dark brown sugar

4 tablespoons minced garlic

¼ cup melted unsalted butter

Freshly ground black pepper

3 tablespoons grapeseed or canola oil

2 pints Brussels sprouts, halved and cored

10 new potatoes, halved

2 tablespoons naturally brewed ponzu

Pork is my favorite meat—and fillets cut from the loin are a great way to enjoy it. The meat's sweetness is yin to the yang of chile in this delicious recipe, which also features garlicky Brussels sprouts. I wasn't always a fan of that vegetable, but now I am, having enjoyed them properly prepared, as they are here. Cooked until just done, the sprouts have a delicate cabbage flavor that even kids will love. This versatile dish works for family and company alike.

1. At least 2 and up to 4 hours in advance, brine the pork: In a bowl large enough to hold the pork and brine, combine the ⅓ cup salt, the sugar, and 8 cups of water. Stir to dissolve the salt and sugar and add the pork. If the pork isn't covered, add more water. Refrigerate for 2 to 4 hours. Rinse the pork and pat dry.

2. Preheat the oven to 350°F. On a large shallow plate combine the chile powder, brown sugar, 2 tablespoons of the garlic, and the butter and blend. Roll the pork in the mixture and season lightly with salt and pepper.

3. Heat a large heavy skillet over medium heat. Add 2 tablespoons of the oil and swirl to coat the pan. When the oil is hot, add the pork and sauté, turning once, until brown, about 6 minutes. Transfer the pork to a plate and set aside.

4. Add the remaining tablespoon of oil to the skillet, swirl, and when hot, add the Brussels sprouts, potatoes, remaining garlic, and ponzu. Season with salt and pepper and mix well. Top with the pork and roast in the oven until the pork is medium, with an internal temperature of 140°F, 15 to 20 minutes. Remove and allow to rest 10 minutes.

5. Transfer the sprouts and potatoes to four individual plates, top with the pork, and serve. Alternatively, transfer the pork to a cutting pork and slice. Distribute the vegetables and sliced pork to four individual serving plates and serve.

five-spice honey pork tenderloin with leeks

TO DRINK:
A French Pinot Noir, like
Méo-Camuzet

Pork is surely the sweetest meat—and the honey-mustard glaze given it in this recipe enhances that pleasing virtue. Leeks, which I think of as French scallions, add a subtle sweetness of their own, and five-spice powder, often used with pork in Chinese cooking, adds its distinctive warmth. This delicious dish is perfect for entertaining.

[Serves 4]

2 medium pork tenderloins (about 2 pounds), any silverskin removed

$^1/_3$ cup kosher salt, for brining, plus more for seasoning

$^1/_4$ cup sugar

2 large leeks, white parts cut into $^1/_2$-inch dice, well washed and dried (see Ming's Tip on washing, page 47)

Freshly ground black pepper

1 teaspoon five-spice powder

2 tablespoons Dijon mustard

$^1/_2$ cup honey

2 tablespoons grapeseed or canola oil

2 tablespoons extra-virgin olive oil

3 cups cooked wild rice (see page 12)

$^1/_2$ cup fresh chicken stock or low-sodium canned chicken broth

1. At least 2 and up to 4 hours in advance, brine the pork: In a bowl large enough to hold the pork and brine, combine the $^1/_3$ cup salt, the sugar and 8 cups of water. Stir to dissolve the salt and sugar, and add the pork. If the pork isn't covered, add more water. Refrigerate for 2 to 4 hours.

2. Preheat the oven to 400°F. Season the leeks with salt and pepper and transfer to a medium bowl. In a small bowl, combine the five-spice powder, mustard and honey. Pour about one third of the mixture into a second small bowl and set both bowls aside.

3. Rinse the pork well, pat dry, and season lightly with salt and more generously with pepper. Heat a large heavy ovenproof skillet over high heat. Add the grapeseed oil and swirl to coat the bottom. When the oil is hot, add the pork and sauté on all sides until brown, about 8 minutes. Transfer the pork to a plate.

4. Add the olive oil to the skillet, swirl, and when hot, add the leeks. Sauté, stirring, until soft, about 3 minutes. Add the rice and stock to the pan and stir. Top with the pork, brush with some of the larger quantity of the honey glaze, and roast the pork for 10 minutes. Turn the pork, brush again with the glaze, and roast until just cooked through, 10 to 15 minutes, or to an internal temperature of 150°F. (Alternatively, insert a paring knife into the thickest part of the meat. If the juices run clear and the knife feels hot, the pork is done.)

5. Transfer the pork to a carving board and allow to rest 8 to 10 minutes. Slice the pork $^1/_4$ inch thick. Transfer the leek mixture to a platter, top with the pork, drizzle with the reserved glaze, and serve.

peppered pork tenderloin with coconut cranberry sauce

It's no secret that pork and fruit make a great duo. This dish pairs peppery pork with extra-tart dried cranberries and ponzu and adds the taste of coconut. I use coconut milk here because it provides richness as well as great flavor. In fact, whenever I'm about to reach for cream to add to a dish, I think coconut milk, and I often use it instead. It has the same mouthfeel as cream and adds exotic flavor. This is another perfect dish for entertaining.

1. At least 2 and up to 4 hours in advance, brine the pork: In a bowl large enough to hold the pork and brine, combine the ⅓ cup salt, the sugar, and 8 cups of water. Stir to dissolve the salt and sugar, and add the pork. If the pork isn't covered, add more water and refrigerate for 2 to 4 hours.

2. Preheat the oven to 450°F. Bake the sweet potatoes until they are soft, about 40 minutes. Do not turn off the oven.

3. About 15 minutes before the potatoes are done, rinse the pork and pat dry. Season lightly with salt and coat with the pepper. Heat a medium sauté pan over medium heat. Add the oil and swirl to coat the bottom. When the oil is hot, add the pork and sauté on all sides, 2 to 3 minutes. Transfer the pan to the oven and roast for 6 to 8 minutes for medium or to an internal temperature of 150°F. (You can also determine doneness by inserting a knife into the thickest part of the pork; see Ming's Tip, page 118.) Remove the pork to a cutting board and let rest.

4. Add a touch more oil to the pan and swirl to coat the bottom. When the oil is hot, add the onions and dried cranberries and sauté, stirring, until the onions have browned lightly, 4 to 5 minutes. Add the ponzu, deglaze, and reduce the liquid by half, about 1 minute. Whisk in the coconut milk and butter and season with salt and pepper.

5. Cut the pork into 12 slices. Divide the sauce among four individual serving plates. Scoop out the potato from its skin and divide it among the plates. Surround each scoop of potato with 3 slices of pork and serve.

TO DRINK:
A crisp, off-dry Riesling, like Rocky Gully Dry from Australia

[Serves 4]

2 medium pork tenderloins (about 2 pounds), any silverskin removed

⅓ cup kosher salt, for brining, plus more for seasoning

¼ cup sugar

2 medium sweet potatoes

2 tablespoons coarsely ground black pepper

2 tablespoons grapeseed or canola oil, plus more as needed

1 large red onion, minced

½ cup coarsely chopped dried cranberries, preferably Craisins

½ cup naturally brewed ponzu

One 14-ounce can coconut milk, shaken

1 tablespoon unsalted butter

TO DRINK:
A chilled India Pale Ale like Samuel Adams or Harpoon

[Serves 4]

Kosher salt

2 cups Israeli couscous

1 tablespoon minced garlic

1 tablespoon minced ginger

1 teaspoon sambal or other hot sauce

1/4 cup hoisin sauce

Zest and juice of 1 large lemon

Two 14-ounce packages firm tofu, quartered lengthwise

1/4 cup extra-virgin olive oil

1 large summer squash, cut into 1/8-inch slices

1 large tomato, cut into 1/4-inch dice

1 bunch scallions, white and green parts, sliced thin

Freshly ground black pepper

barbecued tofu with israeli couscous salad

Barbecuing isn't just for hamburgers. For this easy dish, tofu is brushed with a garlicky hoisin-based "barbecue sauce" then broiled until the surface is deliciously caramelized. I pair the tofu with Israeli couscous, which, if you haven't tried it, is pearl-grained and has a satisfying tender-chewy texture. The couscous is enlivened with thinly sliced raw squash, scallions and tomatoes and is served with the glazed tofu on top.

1. To make the couscous, bring 4 cups of salted water to a boil in a medium saucepan. Stir in the couscous, lower the heat to medium, and cook, stirring frequently, until the couscous is tender, 5 to 10 minutes. Remove from the heat, transfer to a large strainer, and cool under cold running water. Set aside.

2. Preheat the broiler. In a large bowl, combine the garlic, ginger, sambal, hoisin and lemon zest and stir to blend. Place the tofu on a baking sheet and brush generously with the hoisin mixture. Transfer the remaining hoisin mixture to a large bowl.

3. Broil the tofu at middle level until the surface has caramelized and the tofu is heated through, about 6 minutes.

4. Meanwhile, whisk the oil and lemon juice into the reserved hoisin mixture. Add the squash, tomato, scallions and couscous, toss, and season with salt and pepper. Transfer the salad to four individual serving plates, top each portion with 2 parallel slices of tofu, and serve.

5

My high-temperature cooking involves two techniques: flash-frying and steaming. These one-pot methods differ from other stovetop techniques in the way that heat is transferred to raw ingredients—indirectly, that is, via vapor or hot oil. I'm particularly fond of high-temp recipes, as they produce some of cooking's most delectable dishes. Everyone loves crunch, and "hot oil" dishes such as Spicy Fried Chicken and Flash-Fried Eggplant with Honey-Lemon Syrup definitely prove the point.

Steaming is an underexplored technique in the West, but not in the East, where it's used in deliciously creative ways to produce dishes of fresh taste and appearance. The Chinese in particular have recognized the potential for "one-pot" steaming, employing multi-tiered bamboo steamers to cook separate ingredients at once. My steamed recipes, like Lion's Head and Snow Cabbage with Brown Rice, reveal the deep pleasures—and convenience—of steam cooking. In fact, if I had my way, I'd make sure every household had a steamer and used it. Once you crank it up and add your ingredients, a delicious meal is just minutes away.

HIGH TEMP

spicy fried chicken with crispy onion rings

Whenever I eat in the South, I marvel at the number of ways chicken can be fried. Being a chef, I set out to make my own "best" version. This is it—spicy, crisp and delicious, and super-moist because the bird is brined in buttermilk before frying. And you get crispy onion rings with your chicken, so the best's even better.

1. Brine the chicken a day in advance: Mix the ½ cup salt, sugar and buttermilk in a large bowl and stir to dissolve the sugar. Add the chicken, cover, and refrigerate. Four hours before frying, add the onion rings, cover, and refrigerate.

2. Remove the chicken from the brine and drain the onion rings on paper towels. Reserve the brine.

3. Set up a fryer or use a stockpot or other tall wide pot. Add 1 inch of the oil and heat to 325°F, as measured with a deep-fat thermometer. Meanwhile, on a large platter combine the chile flakes, garlic and onion powders, paprika, cornstarch and flour. Dredge the chicken in the cornstarch mixture. Reserve the mixture.

4. Working in batches, shake any excess cornstarch mixture from the chicken. Using a skimmer or tongs, lower the chicken into the oil. Fry the chicken until golden brown and cooked through, turning as needed, 12 to 14 minutes. Remove from the oil, season with salt, and keep warm.

5. Allow the oil to reheat. Dredge the onion in the reserved flour mixture, dip in the brine, and dredge again in the flour mixture. Add the onion rings to the oil and fry until golden brown, about 3 minutes. Drain the rings on paper towels and season lightly with salt. Transfer the chicken and onion rings to four individual serving plates and serve with the lemon for squeezing over.

TO DRINK:
Yangjing beer or other light, crisp lagers, such as Michelob Ultra, Corona, or Stella Artois

[Serves 4]

½ cup kosher salt for brining, plus more for seasoning

½ cup sugar

1 quart buttermilk

6 chicken legs and 6 thighs

1 large onion, cut into ½-inch slices

Grapeseed or canola oil, for frying

2 tablespoons Korean chile pepper flakes or chili powder

2 tablespoons natural garlic powder

2 tablespoons onion powder

1 tablespoon paprika

2 cups cornstarch

2 cups all-purpose flour

1 lemon, quartered

Ming's Tip:
Salt the bird right after it's fried or the seasoning won't stick. And to ensure even salting, "rain" it on the bird from shoulder height.

panko-crusted turkey "scaloppini" with warm mango-cranberry chutney

TO DRINK:
A Dolcetto d'Alba, like Roberto Voerzio from Italy

I'm a great fan of turkey and constantly looking for new ways to serve it other than roasted. When making veal scaloppini one day, I suddenly wondered if I could substitute turkey for the veal. Turns out, turkey does beautifully pounded into thin slices, coated with bread crumbs—here, Japanese panko—and quickly sautéed. When accompanied by warm mango-cranberry chutney, a recasting of the usual cranberry sauce, the scaloppini really shine.

[Serves 4]

2 pounds skinless turkey breast, cut on the extreme bias into 8 slices about 8 inches long and 1/2 inch thick

Kosher salt and freshly ground black pepper

2 eggs

1 cup panko (Japanese bread crumbs)

1/2 cup finely chopped parsley

1 cup all-purpose flour

5 tablespoons extra-virgin olive oil

2 shallots, minced

1 cup fresh cranberries, washed and dried

1 large mango, peeled and cut into 1/2-inch dice

1 tablespoon Dijon mustard

1. Place a turkey portion on a work surface and cover with plastic wrap. Using a pounder or small sauté pan, pound the turkey until 1/4 inch thick. Repeat with the remaining portions. Season the turkey on both sides with salt and pepper.

2. In a shallow bowl, beat the eggs lightly. On a large plate, combine the panko and half the parsley. Spread the flour on a second plate.

3. One by one, coat the turkey portions lightly with the flour, dip them into the egg, and then coat with the panko mixture.

4. Line a large plate with paper towels. Heat a large sauté pan over medium-high heat. Add 2 tablespoons of the oil and swirl to coat the bottom. When the oil is hot, add half the turkey slices and sauté, turning once, until golden brown and cooked through, 6 to 8 minutes. Transfer the turkey to the plate. Repeat using 2 more tablespoons of the oil.

5. Wipe out the pan with a paper towel and add the remaining tablespoon of oil. Swirl to coat the bottom and when the oil is hot, add the shallots and sauté until soft, about 1 minute. Add the cranberries, mango and mustard and sauté, stirring, until the fruit is soft, about 2 minutes. Add the remaining parsley and stir to combine.

6. Transfer 2 scaloppini to each of four individual serving plates. Dollop some chutney on the side, and serve.

TO DRINK:
A spicy dry Riesling, like Lucien Albrecht Reserve from France

[Serves 4]

1½ pounds pork shoulder, cut into 1-inch cubes

Kosher salt and freshly ground black pepper

1 cup cornstarch

½ cup grapeseed or canola oil

½ cup naturally brewed rice vinegar

1 to 3 tablespoons sugar, depending on the mangoes' sweetness

1 bunch scallions, sliced thin, white and green parts separated

1 tablespoon minced garlic

1 tablespoon minced ginger

1 medium red onion, cut into ¼-inch dice

2 small mangoes, peeled and cut into ½-inch dice

1 red bell pepper, cut into ¼-inch dice

¼ cup tablespoons naturally brewed soy sauce

–

50-50 White and Brown Rice, for serving (see page 12)

sweet and sour mango pork

Almost anyone who's ever eaten Chinese food in America has had sweet and sour pork. Here's my tropical version, which should be a revelation to those who haven't always loved the dish. The key here is flash-frying the pork before combining it with the other ingredients, a technique that gives the meat crispness. Mango provides tropical allure, but if you can't find mangoes that are ripe, or if they're out of season, substitute a small pineapple. The result will be less exotic but just as good.

1. Season the pork with salt and pepper. Spread the cornstarch on a platter and dredge the pork thoroughly on all sides.

2. Line a large plate with paper towels. Heat a wok over high heat. Add the oil and swirl to coat the pan. When the oil is hot, add half the pork and fry, turning the pork, until brown, about 4 minutes. Using a skimmer, transfer the pork to the lined plate to drain. Fry the remaining pork and it transfer to the plate. Pour off all but 1 tablespoon of the oil from the wok.

3. In a small bowl, combine the vinegar and sugar and stir to dissolve the sugar. Set aside.

4. Return the wok to medium-high heat and when the oil is hot, add the scallion whites, garlic, ginger and onions and stir-fry until softened, about 1 minute. And the mangoes, bell pepper, soy sauce and vinegar mixture and bring to a simmer. Return the pork to the wok and mix thoroughly.

5. Transfer the stir-fry to a platter and serve with the rice.

lion's head and snow cabbage with house rice

Chinese dishes have evocative names. The lion's head of this recipe title refers to plus-size meatballs, here a savory mixture of ground beef and pork, and the snow cabbage represents the mane. My grandfather would prepare the traditional version of this dish, which I've made even more savory by adding, among other things, Worcestershire sauce, an under-appreciated seasoning. A final touch of sambal provides heat.

1. Set up a steamer, using an elevated bamboo steamer in a water-filled wok, a collapsible steamer well elevated above water, or a commercial steamer with pot and steamer insert.

2. In a large bowl, combine the pork, beef, onions, garlic, ginger, Worcestershire sauce, sesame oil, rice and eggs. Season with salt and pepper and mix by hand until just combined. Check the seasoning by sautéing a small amount of the mixture, or use a microwave to cook it (about 10 seconds at high power).

3. Using your hands, lightly form the mixture into 2-inch balls. Place a ¾- to 1-inch bed of the cabbage in the top of the steamer and top with the meatballs. Season with salt and pepper and steam until the meatballs and cabbage are cooked through, 8 to 10 minutes. Transfer the cabbage to a platter or four serving plates, top with the meatballs, garnish with a bit of sambal, and serve.

TO DRINK:
A light fruity red, like Domaine La Manarine Côtes du Rhone from France

[Serves 4]

¾ pound ground pork

¾ pound ground beef

1 medium onion, cut into ¼-inch dice

1 tablespoon minced garlic

2 tablespoons minced ginger

2 tablespoons Worcestershire sauce

1 tablespoon toasted sesame oil

1 cup 50-50 White and Brown Rice (see page 12); save extra rice for another use

2 large eggs

Kosher salt and freshly ground black pepper

1 small head napa cabbage, cut into very thin strips

1 tablespoon sambal, for garnish

Ming's Tip:
To ease meatball making, wet your hands first.

TO DRINK:
An unoaked Chardonnay like
Elderton from the Barossa Valley
in Australia

[Serves 4]

1 banana leaf, 2 kale or iceberg lettuce
leaves, or parchment paper cut to fit the
steamer top

Four 6-ounce arctic char fillets with skin,
scaled

Kosher salt and freshly ground black pepper

1 tablespoon very thin strips peeled ginger

2 limes, halved and cut into 1/4-inch-thick
half-moons

2 tablespoons naturally brewed soy sauce,
plus more for drizzling

1/4 cup grapeseed or canola oil

soy-lime steamed arctic char with grapeseed-oil flash

Finishing a dish with a drizzle of hot oil is an easy Chinese technique that gives steamed fish just the right touch of richness. Here, arctic char is steamed simply with lime slices, soy sauce, and ginger then finished with the oil. You get the clean tastiness of the fish, which couldn't be better for you, plus great flavor. The fillets are cooked skin-on. The skin is nutritious, but you can remove it, if you like. I love my fish on the rare side, but if you don't, steam the fillets until just cooked through.

1. Set up a steamer. Place the banana leaf or other leaf or paper in the top part.

2. Season the fillets lightly with salt and pepper and transfer to the steamer skin side down. Sprinkle evenly with the ginger and top with the lime. Drizzle with the 2 tablespoons of soy sauce and steam until the fillets are medium-rare, 8 to 10 minutes, or just cooked through, 10 to 12 minutes.

3. Meanwhile, in a small saucepan heat the oil to the smoking point. Very carefully, standing back to avoid splatters, use a tablespoon to spoon the hot oil over the cooked fillets in the steamer. If using a bamboo steamer, serve from it. Otherwise, transfer the fillets with the banana leaf, or alone if other leaves or parchment paper were used, to a platter. Drizzle with the soy sauce and serve.

Ming's Tip:

When shopping for fish, make sure to check it for absolute freshness. The fish should look naturally moist, without a bit of dryness. If whole, look for red gills, intact scales, and no surface browning. No matter the cut, fish should smell fresh, like the sea. Ask your fish seller to put a potential purchase on a piece of paper so you can give it a sniff. If he or she objects, shop elsewhere!

flash-fried eggplant with honey-lemon syrup

TO DRINK:
Veuve Clicquot Champagne

[Serves 4]

1 large eggplant, cut into 1/4-inch slices

Kosher salt and freshly ground black pepper

1/4 cup honey

1 tablespoon naturally brewed soy sauce

Zest from 1 lemon, plus 1 tablespoon juice

5 scallions, sliced thin, white and green parts separated, 2 tablespoons of the greens reserved for garnish

2 large eggs

2 cups panko (Japanese bread crumbs)

1 cup all-purpose flour

Grapeseed or canola oil, for flash-frying

If you're a fan of eggplant—and even if you're not—you'll love this dish. Sliced thin and flash-fried, eggplant is transformed into the best (not to mention largest) chips you've ever had. Partnered by syrup inspired by the traditional Middle Eastern lemon and honey pairing, this starts any meal with a major bang.

1. Place the eggplant on a plate and salt generously. Let stand for 1 hour to release its liquid and any bitterness. Rinse well, pat dry, season with pepper, and set aside.

2. In a small bowl, combine the honey, soy sauce, lemon zest and juice, and the larger quantity of scallion greens.

3. Beat the eggs in a large shallow soup plate. Combine the panko and scallion whites on a large plate. Spread the flour on a second large plate. Dredge the eggplant it the flour, shake off any excess, dip it in the eggs, and then dredge in the panko mixture.

4. Fill a large high-sided skillet with 1/2 inch of the oil and heat over medium heat to 350°F, as measured with a deep-fat thermometer. Working in batches, if necessary, fry the eggplant until golden brown, 2 to 3 minutes. Drain the eggplant on a paper-towel–lined plate.

5. Stack the eggplant chips on a serving plate, drizzle with the syrup, garnish with the remaining scallion greens, and serve.

TO DRINK:
A crisp lager like Yanjing from China

crispy tofu with miso butter and iceberg lettuce

[Serves 4]

2 tablespoons shiro miso

2 tablespoons naturally brewed ponzu, plus more for drizzling

¼ pound salted butter, at room temperature

Grapeseed or canola oil, for frying

Two 12-ounce packages silken tofu, each portion quartered lengthwise

1 tablespoon togarashi or chili powder

Kosher salt and freshly ground black pepper

2 cups rice flour

½ head iceberg lettuce, shredded

2 tablespoons finely sliced chives, for garnish

This recipe elevates humble yet healthful tofu to great, delicious heights. It's flash-fried, which makes it golden brown and crispy. The tofu's then dolloped with a flavorful miso butter whose richness is offset by ponzu and iceberg lettuce—a lettuce I've always loved for its compatible, no-frills crunchiness. This makes a great light meal or appetizer.

1. In a medium bowl, combine the miso and ponzu. Using a hand blender or sturdy whisk, whip until well blended. Add the butter and whip until blended. Set aside.

2. Fill a heavy medium skillet ½ inch full with the oil. Heat over medium heat to 375°F.

3. Meanwhile, season the tofu with the togarashi and salt and pepper to taste. Spread the rice flour on a large plate, add the tofu, and dredge on all sides. Shake off excess flour and, using a skimmer or slotted spatula, transfer half the tofu to the oil. Fry the tofu until crisp, turning once, 2 to 3 minutes. Drain on paper towels. Repeat with the remaining tofu.

4. Transfer the lettuce to a platter or divide the lettuce among four serving plates. Drizzle with the ponzu, top with the tofu, and dollop with the butter mixture. Garnish with the chives and serve.

Ming's Tips:

The frying is best done in a heavy, straight-sided pan, but any heavy pan will do. You may have extra miso butter. Refrigerate it and use it later for searing fish or meat.

6

Soup is the ultimate one-pot dish—and undoubtedly the original. Its preparation is as basic as the satisfaction it delivers. You put ingredients in a pot, add liquid, and simmer. Hours later—soup.

As easy as it is to prepare, though, there are soups and soups. I've made sure that the ones in this chapter, like Wonton Shrimp and Noodle Soup and Beef and Onion "Sukiyaki," are both convenient and delicious. Soups can be hearty and stew-like, such as Mussel and Rice Stew, or delicate and more dressed up, such as New-Style Halibut Sashimi Soup, a lovely, rave-getting starter. Soup is also one of the dishes most likely to make meat eaters shake hands with vegetarians: both will love my Five-Vegetable Miso Stew and Three Bean Chile, as well as my takes on traditional favorites, like Lemongrass-Coconut Chicken Soup, based on the Thai *tom yung gai*, and Shrimp Bouillabaisse. Soup is beloved by all—and one-pot easy, too.

SOUP

lemongrass-coconut chicken soup

This light but deliciously fortifying soup is based on the Thai classic, *tom yung gai*. It features what I think of as the defining Thai flavoring, lemongrass, combined with chicken, coconut milk, and chiles, for heat. I've followed the time-honored Thai approach of leaving whole pieces of the lemongrass in the soup, but you can strain them out, if you like. (If you do leave them in, tell diners not to eat them.) This makes a great starter, of course, but is also terrific as a light meal accompanied by a salad dressed with citrus vinaigrette.

1. Heat a medium saucepan over medium heat. Add the oil and swirl to coat the bottom. When the oil is hot, add the lemongrass and sauté, stirring, for 2 minutes. Add the celery, carrots, onions and chiles, if using, and sauté, stirring, for 1 minute. Season with salt and pepper.

2. Add the chicken and sauté until opaque, about 1 minute. Add the fish sauce and stock, stir, bring to a simmer, and cook until the liquid is reduced by one fifth, about 5 minutes. Add the coconut milk and lemon juice and stir. Add the basil and adjust the seasoning, if necessary. Serve.

TO DRINK:
A full-bodied Sauvignon Blanc, like Château Carbonnieux Grand Cru Classé de Graves from France

[Serves 4]

1 tablespoon grapeseed or canola oil

4 lemongrass stalks, pale parts only, crushed with the flat side of a knife

1 head celery, stalks rinsed and roughly chopped

2 large carrots, peeled and shredded

2 medium onions, thinly sliced

2 Thai or serrano chiles, stemmed and minced (optional)

Kosher salt and freshly ground black pepper

2 boneless, skinless chicken breasts, cut widthwise into 1/4-inch strips

3 tablespoons fish sauce

6 cups unsalted fresh chicken stock or low-sodium canned chicken broth

1/4 cup coconut milk

Juice of 1 lemon

1/4 cup whole Thai basil leaves, or regular basil

beef and onion "sukiyaki"

TO DRINK:
A clean Japanese beer like
Kirin, Saporo, or Asahi

[Serves 4]

8 ounces rice stick noodles

1 tablespoon grapeseed or canola oil

3 large onions, halved and cut into
1/4-inch slices

1 tablespoon minced ginger

1/2 cup mirin

2 quarts fresh chicken stock or low-sodium
canned chicken broth

2 tablespoons naturally brewed soy sauce

Kosher salt and freshly ground black pepper

1 pound beef tenderloin, sliced paper thin
(see headnote)

This soupy, soul-satisfying dish is based on sukiyaki, a dish I first enjoyed in its home country, Japan. Like that dish, this one can be finished at the table, which makes it good for a special occasion, or for creating one. Here, paper-thin slices of beef—have your butcher do the cutting—are floated on the top of a steaming, noodle-filled broth, where they cook very quickly. You can substitute thinly sliced chicken for the beef, if you like, but whichever the meat, you'll enjoy a deliciously slurpy meal.

1. Place the noodles in a large bowl and cover them generously with hot water. Soak until soft, about 20 minutes. Drain and set aside.

2. Heat a large deep skillet over high heat. Add the oil and swirl to coat the bottom. When the oil is hot, add the onions and ginger and sauté, stirring, until the onions have browned, about 5 minutes. Add the mirin, deglaze the pan, and reduce by one quarter, about 3 minutes. Add the stock, reduce the heat to medium, and simmer until the liquid has reduced slightly, about 10 minutes. Add the noodles and soy sauce and season with salt and pepper.

3. Using chopsticks or tongs, float the beef on the surface of the liquid until just cooked through, turning it once. It will be cooked in about 1 minute. Divide the beef, soup and noodles among heated bowls and serve with soup spoons and chopsticks.

Ming's Tip:
If you own a large, high-sided sauté pan—what the French call a "sautoir"—you can cook the dish in it and bring it to the table.

miso-butter pork ramen-noodle soup

I grew up eating—and loving—Chinese noodle soups. Fast-forward to my culinary training in Japan, where I came to adore miso-flavored broths with ramen noodles. My version borrows the hearty depth of those miso-laced soups and features the rich meatiness of pork. A bit of butter—definitely a Western touch—rounds everything out. I can't imagine an appetite this wouldn't satisfy, particularly on a cold day.

1. Fill a large bowl with water and add ice cubes. In a stockpot or other tall wide pot, cook the noodles in abundant boiling salted water for 2 to 3 minutes if fresh, 6 to 8 minutes if dry. Drain the noodles and transfer to the ice water. When cold, drain and set aside.

2. Heat the same pot over medium heat. Add the oil and swirl to coat the bottom. When the oil is hot add the shallots, ginger and pork and sauté, breaking up the pork, until the meat is cooked through, 3 to 4 minutes. Add the scallion whites and mirin, deglaze, and simmer until the liquid is reduced by half, 1 to 2 minutes. Add the stock and the apples and bring to a simmer.

3. Whisk in the butter and the miso and season with salt and pepper. Add the reserved noodles and heat through, about 2 minutes. Divide the noodles and soup among four individual bowls, garnish with the scallion greens, and serve.

TO DRINK:
A dry Japanese beer
like Kirin or Asahi

[Serves 4]

1 pound fresh or dried ramen noodles

Kosher salt

2 tablespoons grapeseed or canola oil

3 shallots, minced

1 tablespoon minced ginger

1 pound ground pork

1 bunch scallions, thinly sliced, green and white parts separated

1/2 cup mirin

2 quarts fresh chicken stock or low-sodium canned chicken broth

2 Red Delicious apples, peeled, cored, and thinly sliced

4 tablespoons (1/2 sticks) unsalted butter

6 tablespoons shiro miso

Freshly ground black pepper

shrimp bouillabaisse

TO DRINK:
A chilled rosé, like Tavel

Traditional bouillabaisse is a marvelous dish that requires many kinds of seafood and a lot of time to make. My quicker version delivers all the thrills of the original but uses only shrimp, plus fennel and edamame. Yogurt adds a sense of the characteristic creaminess, and buttery garlic bread completes the meal.

1. Heat a stockpot or other tall wide pot over high heat. Add 2 tablespoons of the oil and swirl to coat the bottom. When the oil is hot, add the shrimp shells and sauté, stirring, until the shells have turned pink, 1 to 2 minutes. Add the wine, deglaze the pot, and reduce the liquid by half, 1 to 2 minutes. Add the stock, season with salt and pepper, and simmer until the liquid is reduced by one quarter, 5 to 6 minutes. Strain the liquid and transfer to a large bowl. Set aside. (Discard the shells.)

2. Preheat the broiler. Dry out the pot and heat over medium-high heat. Add the remaining tablespoon oil and swirl to coat the bottom. When the oil is hot, add the fennel, onions, carrot, celery and paprika. Season with salt and pepper and sauté until the vegetables are soft, about 3 minutes. Add the strained stock, shrimp and edamame, and simmer until the shrimp are just cooked through, about 3 minutes. Whisk in the yogurt and adjust the seasoning, if necessary.

3. Meanwhile, in a small bowl combine the butter and garlic. Season with salt and pepper, blend, and spread on one side of the bread slices. Transfer to a large broiling pan and broil at the middle level until the bread is golden, 2 to 3 minutes. Watch carefully to ensure the bread doesn't burn.

4. Ladle the soup into four individual serving bowls and serve with the bread.

[Serves 4]

3 tablespoons grapeseed or canola oil

1½ pounds medium (U 13-15) shrimp, peeled, deveined, and halved lengthwise, shells reserved

1 cup dry white wine

2 quarts fresh chicken stock or low-sodium canned chicken broth

Kosher salt and freshly ground black pepper

1 small fennel bulb, halved, cored, and cut into ½-inch dice

1 medium onion, cut into ¼-inch dice

1 large carrot, peeled and cut into ¼-inch dice

2 celery stalks, cut into ¼-inch dice

1 tablespoon paprika

1 cup shelled edamame

1 cup Greek yogurt

4 tablespoons (½ stick) unsalted butter, softened

1 tablespoon minced garlic

1 baguette, cut on the bias into ½-inch slices

TO DRINK:
A Riesling, like P.J. Valkenberg
Estate Kabinett from Germany

[Serves 4]

1 tablespoon unsalted butter

2 tablespoons very fine strips peeled ginger

1 medium onion, halved lengthwise and thinly sliced

1 bunch scallions, thinly sliced, white and green parts separated

Kosher salt and freshly ground black pepper

1 quart fresh chicken stock or low-sodium canned chicken broth

One 4-ounce piece halibut, cut into ¼-inch slices

Pinches of togarashi (see page 11) or chile pepper flakes, for garnish

2 sheets nori (dried seaweed), folded lengthwise 6 times, then cut widthwise with scissors into ⅛-inch strips

new-style halibut sashimi soup

This is by far the lightest and most delicate recipe in this book—and a fantastic way to start a meal. You make a delicious broth that's topped by pristine slices of raw halibut. The halibut is partially cooked by the hot liquid, and it retains the texture of sashimi. Ribbons of nori and a sprinkling of chile pepper flakes complete the presentation, which is especially memorable if you do the final soup ladling at the table.

1. Heat a large saucepan over low heat. Add the butter and when hot, add the ginger, onions, and scallion whites. Sauté, stirring, until soft, 1 to 2 minutes. Season with salt and pepper. Add the stock and bring to a simmer. Reduce the heat and simmer until the stock is reduced by one quarter, 3 to 4 minutes.

2. Using a skimmer, remove the onions and ginger from the stock and transfer to four individual serving bowls. Top each with the halibut slices. Sprinkle with the togarashi, scallion greens, and nori. Ladle in the broth until it just covers the fish (or for cooked-through fish, cover it with broth) and serve immediately.

Ming's Tip:

To make this dish a success, as well as healthful eating, you must get absolutely fresh, sashimi-grade fish. Once that's taken care of, you'll have a fantastic dish that's also quick to do.

TO DRINK:
An unoaked Chablis-like
Chardonnay like Stony Hill
from California

[Serves 4]

1 tablespoon grapeseed or canola oil

8 garlic cloves, sliced thin

2 shallots, sliced thin

2 slices bacon, cut into 1/4-inch dice

1 large fennel bulb, halved, cored, and sliced 1/4-inch thick

1 pound mussels, preferably Prince Edward Island, cleaned and beards removed, or cultivated mussels

2 cups dry white wine

2 cups fresh chicken stock or low-sodium canned chicken broth

2 cups 50-50 White and Brown Rice (see page 12); save extra rice for another use

1 tablespoon oyster sauce, vegetarian oyster sauce, or wheat-free tamari sauce

Kosher salt and freshly ground black pepper

1 lemon, quartered, for garnish

mussel and rice stew

Different cultures have different takes on breakfast. A traditional Chinese breakfast consists of jook, which is a rice porridge, with all kinds of savory additions, including meat and fish. You might call this "super-jook," as it's made with a brown rice mixture, stock and mussels, plus bacon. You could serve this for breakfast, but it's really meant for later in the day, when you want something comforting after long hours at work.

1. Heat a stockpot or other tall wide pot over high heat. Add the oil and swirl to coat the bottom. When the oil is hot, add the garlic, shallots, bacon and fennel and sauté, stirring, until the vegetables are soft, about 3 minutes. Add the mussels and heat through, stirring, for 2 minutes Add the wine, deglaze the pot, and simmer until the liquid is reduced by half, about 3 minutes. Remove any mussels that haven't opened and discard. Transfer the opened mussels to a bowl and set aside.

2. Add the stock, rice and oyster sauce to the pot. Bring to a simmer and cook until the rice has released its starch and the mixture is stew-like, 15 to 20 minutes. Return the mussels to the pot, heat through, and season with salt and pepper. Transfer the soup to four individual serving bowls and distribute the mussels in each. Serve with the lemon wedges.

wonton shrimp and noodle soup

TO DRINK:
Toasted Brown-Rice Green Tea

Wonton soup is a great favorite, but is laborious to prepare at home as the wontons must be made from scratch. For this delicious, easier version, wontons are replaced by wonton noodles, thin egg pasta. You get satisfying noodle slurp as well as a rich, shrimp-filled broth. I sometimes add handfuls of baby spinach leaves or julienned bok choy to the soup, but it's delicious as is.

1. Fill a large bowl with water and add ice cubes. In a stockpot or other tall wide pot, cook the noodles in abundant boiling salted water until al dente, about 3 minutes. Drain the noodles and transfer to the ice water. When cold, drain and transfer to a medium bowl. Drizzle in oil to coat the pasta lightly and set aside.

2. Heat the pot over high heat. Add the oil and swirl to coat the bottom. When the oil is hot, add the scallion whites, the larger quantity of the greens, the ginger and star anise and sauté until softened, about 1 minute. Add the stock, bring to a simmer, and reduce by one quarter, about 5 minutes. Add the soy sauce, sesame oil, carrots, noodles and shrimp. Simmer until the shrimp are just cooked through, about 3 minutes.

3. Transfer to four individual soup bowls, garnish with the remaining scallion greens, and serve.

[Serves 4]

1/2 pound wonton noodles or angel hair pasta

Kosher salt

1 tablespoon grapeseed or canola oil, plus more for coating the noodles

2 bunches scallions, sliced thin, white and green parts separated, 1/2 cup of greens reserved for garnish

1 tablespoon thinly sliced ginger

1 star anise

2 quarts fresh chicken stock or low-sodium canned chicken broth

2 tablespoons naturally brewed soy sauce

1 tablespoon toasted sesame oil

1 1/2 cups peeled shredded carrots

1 pound small (51-60) shrimp

spicy clam and shrimp soup

This light but deeply flavorful soup borrows from the Thai pantry by using lemongrass, chiles, lime and coconut milk. I've upped the ante, though, by adding clams and shrimp, whose briny sweetness is heightened by the other flavorings. Thai basil adds its own licorice-like appeal. Before cooking, the clams are purged, an unattended soaking process that ensures grit-free eating. If, however, you don't have the time and don't mind the possibility of a bit of grit, you can skip it.

1. Fill a large bowl with water. Add the cornmeal, stir, and add the clams. Let the clams purge for at least 1 hour and up to 3.

2. Meanwhile, heat a stockpot or other tall wide pot over medium heat. Add the oil and swirl to coat the bottom. When the oil is hot add the shallots, chiles, ginger, lime leaves and lemongrass and sauté, stirring, for 1 minute. Add the clams, season lightly with salt and pepper, and cook, stirring occasionally, until the clams start to open, 2 to 3 minutes. Deglaze with the fish sauce and lime juice.

3. Add the chicken stock and basil sprigs, cover, and bring to a simmer. Cook until the clams have opened fully, 4 to 5 minutes (discard any clams that haven't opened). Add the shrimp and coconut milk and simmer until the shrimp are cooked through, about 3 minutes. Transfer to four individual bowls, garnish with the basil leaves, and serve

TO DRINK:
An off-dry Gewürztraminer, like Halleck from California

[Serves 4]

¼ cup cornmeal

1 pound small clams or cockles

1 tablespoon grapeseed or canola oil

4 shallots, sliced thin

2 Thai bird chiles, seeded and thinly sliced

Two ¼-inch-thick slices ginger cut from a 2- to 4-inch piece

6 limes leaves, hand-crushed

2 stalks lemongrass, white part only, crushed with the flat of a knife

Kosher salt and freshly ground black pepper

2 tablespoons fish sauce

Juice of 4 limes

2 quarts fresh chicken stock or low-sodium canned chicken broth

4 sprigs Thai basil, plus 8 leaves for garnish

½ pound small (51-60) shrimp

¼ cup coconut milk

Ming's Tip:

If any clams refuse to open after full cooking, throw them away. But those that open slightly can be coaxed to open farther, and therefore be used, by inserting the tip of a spoon between the shells and prying gently.

vegetarian
hot and sour soup

You don't need pork to make a fabulous hot and sour soup. The secret is having a deeply flavored broth, which you definitely get in this meatless version. You also get three layers of heat, supplied by ginger, jalapeños and white pepper. Very quickly prepared, this makes a bracing starter guaranteed to whet appetites.

1. Heat a stockpot or other tall wide pot over high heat. Add the oil and swirl to coat the bottom. When the oil is hot, add the scallion whites, jalapeños, and ginger, and sauté, stirring, until softened, 1 minute. Add the white pepper, vinegar, soy sauce and stock and bring to a simmer.

2. Add the tofu and enoki, season with more pepper. Transfer to four individual serving bowls, garnish with the scallion greens, and serve.

TO DRINK:
A Gewürztraminer, like Zind
Humbrecht from France

[Serves 4]

1 tablespoon grapeseed or canola oil

2 bunches scallions, sliced thin, white and green parts separated

2 jalapeños, unseeded, sliced thin

2 tablespoons thinly sliced peeled ginger

2 teaspoons finely ground white pepper, plus more

1/2 cup naturally brewed rice vinegar

6 tablespoons naturally brewed soy sauce

2 quarts vegetable stock

Two 12-ounce packages silken tofu, cut lengthwise into 1/4-inch x 1/4-inch strips

Two 31/2- to 4-ounce packages enoki mushrooms, ends trimmed

TO DRINK:
Green Sencha Tea

five-vegetable
miso stew

Choosing to use miso as the flavor base of this delicious stew was a no-brainer. Miso provides as much deep flavor as a meat addition might, and is way better for you. Sweet potatoes, kale, tomatoes and a touch of tamari do the rest. Vegetable stews can be boring, but this one is a second-helping treat.

[Serves 4]

2 tablespoons grapeseed or canola oil

1 bunch scallions, sliced thin, green and white parts separated

1 large onion, minced

1 large sweet potato, cut into ½-inch dice

Kosher salt and freshly ground black pepper

1 tablespoon minced ginger

2 cups roma tomatoes, chopped roughly, with juice from measuring

2 quarts vegetable stock

1 tablespoon wheat-free tamari sauce

¼ cup plus 2 tablespoons miso

3 cups lightly packed stemmed kale leaves cut into ¼-inch strips

Extra-virgin olive oil, for drizzling

2 whole-wheat pitas, toasted and quartered

1. Heat a stockpot or other tall wide pot over medium heat. Add the oil and swirl to coat the bottom. When the oil is hot, add the scallion whites, onions and potatoes, season with salt and pepper, and sauté until the onions have browned lightly, about 5 minutes. Add the ginger, tomatoes with their juice, stock and tamari.

2. Place the miso in a small strainer, submerge it in the stockpot, and whisk it until it has dispersed into the liquid and remove the strainer. Adjust the seasoning, if necessary. Bring the stew to a simmer and cook until the potatoes are soft and the liquid is reduced by a quarter, about 10 minutes. Adjust the seasoning again, if necessary.

3. Add the kale and simmer until soft, 1 to 2 minutes. Taste the seasoning a final time and adjust, if necessary.

4. Transfer the stew to four individual soup bowls. Drizzle with the olive oil and serve with the pita.

7

Once I saw salads as "one-pot" dishes—they're tossed and served in the same bowl—I recognized how convenient they can be. A good thing, because salads are extremely versatile and fill many menu slots. Salads were formerly understood to be "small-plate" dishes only. We now enjoy a vast range of entrée salads, which can be easy and fun to put together. The recipes in this chapter showcase these meal-in-one salads—whether they are recastings of traditional dishes, such as Coriander-Crusted Tuna Salad Niçoise and Tofu Green Goddess Salad, or delicious "inventions" like Spicy Shrimp and Avocado Salad.

I've also enjoyed lightening favorite salads that relied, usually, on a mayo-based dressing. In place of mayo, I use good-for-you Greek yogurt, which provides creaminess without any heaviness. My Seared Salmon and Greek Yogurt Salad headlines the technique. And for special occasions, I offer Tea-Smoked Salmon with Preserved Lemon and Fennel-Couscous Salad, which may sound like a big deal to put together, but it isn't. My one-pot approach gives salads a new—and really convenient—lease on life.

TOSS

sesame chicken cucumber noodle salad

TO DRINK:
A bright, exotic-fruit Sauvignon Blanc, like a Mulderbosch from South Africa

Just about everyone loves sesame noodle salad, including me. This delicious version improves on the traditional one because it uses a mixture of creamy peanut butter and sesame oil in place of the customary sesame paste. The resulting dish is lighter, not only because the noodles are more delicately coated with the dressing, but because there's less of them in relation to the chicken and veggies.

[Serves 4]

8 ounces Chinese egg noodles or other thin noodles or pasta, fresh or dried

Kosher salt

Vegetable oil, for coating the pasta

2 heads baby romaine or 1 head regular romaine lettuce

1 cup creamy peanut butter

2 tablespoons toasted sesame oil

3/4 cup naturally brewed rice vinegar

2 tablespoons Shaoxing wine or dry sherry

1 cup thinly sliced scallions, white and green parts

1 tablespoon sambal, any kind, or hot sauce

2 tablespoons naturally brewed soy sauce

1/4 cup chopped cilantro (optional)

3 large cooked boneless skinless chicken breasts (about 1 1/2 pounds), cut lengthwise into 1/4-inch slices and chilled

1 large English cucumber, peeled, seeded, halved lengthwise, and cut into 1/4-inch slices

2 medium red bell peppers, cut into 1/4-inch dice

Freshly ground black pepper

Toasted sesame seeds, for garnish

1. Fill a large bowl with water and add ice cubes. Cook the noodles in abundant boiling salted water until al dente, 2 to 4 minutes if fresh, about 6 minutes if dry. Drain and transfer the noodles to the ice water. When the noodles are cold, drain and coat lightly with vegetable oil. Set aside.

2. If using baby romaine, half lengthwise, notch out the core, and cut widthwise into 1/2-inch pieces. If using regular romaine, remove the tougher outer leaves. Halve lengthwise, notch out the core, halve again, and cut widthwise into 1/2-inch pieces. Set aside.

3. For the dressing, in a large bowl whisk together the peanut butter, sesame oil, vinegar and wine. Add the scallions, sambal, soy sauce and cilantro, if using, and stir to blend. Transfer the dressing to a small bowl.

4. In the first bowl, combine the chicken, cucumber, bell peppers, lettuce and noodles. Add three quarters of the dressing and toss. Season with salt and black pepper. Add the remaining dressing if necessary.

5. Transfer the salad to a serving bowl. Garnish with the sesame seeds and serve.

Ming's Tip:

I always cook extra noodles when making this dish. Cooked noodles, stored in the refrigerator, can be turned rapidly into a tasty pan-fried noodle cake or chow mein.

coriander-crusted tuna salad niçoise

I've always enjoyed composed salads—salads with multiple ingredients artfully arranged. Among these, salade Niçoise is probably the best known and most widely enjoyed. It features tuna—traditionally, canned albacore. I've "upped" the dish by using fresh, coriander-coated tuna that's quickly sautéed, plus frisée dressed with a sprightly caper-and-olive-laced vinaigrette. This is a great outdoor dish, perfect for a summer lunch.

1. To hard-boil the eggs, bring enough water to cover the eggs to a boil in a medium saucepan. Lower the eggs into the water and immediately reduce the heat to a simmer. Simmer for 14 minutes and transfer the eggs to cold water. When cold, peel and slice the eggs 1/4 inch thick. Set aside.

2. Make the vinaigrette: In a small bowl combine the mustard, shallots, ponzu, sesame oil, capers and olives and whisk to blend. Slowly whisk in the 1/2 cup of olive oil and season with salt and pepper. Set aside.

3. Season the tuna with salt and pepper on both sides. Spread the coriander on a large plate and press the tuna into it on all sides.

4. Heat a medium sauté pan over medium-high heat. Make sure the pan is very hot. Add the tablespoon of olive oil and swirl to coat the bottom. When the oil is hot, add the tuna and sauté on all sides until medium-rare, about 4 minutes. Remove the tuna and set aside.

5. In a large bowl, combine the frisée and eggs. Season with salt and pepper. Toss gently with the vinaigrette, reserving some for drizzling.

6. Divide the salad among four individual serving plates, top with the tuna, drizzle with the remaining vinaigrette, and serve.

TO DRINK:
A crisp, fruit-forward Sancerre like Lucien Crochet from France

[Serves 4]

2 large eggs

2 tablespoons Dijon mustard

2 tablespoons minced shallots

1/4 cup naturally brewed ponzu

1 tablespoon toasted sesame oil

2 tablespoons chopped capers

2 tablespoons chopped pitted Niçoise olives

1/2 cup plus 1 tablespoon extra-virgin olive oil

Kosher salt and freshly ground black pepper

1 pound center-cut tuna steak, preferably bigeye, cut lengthwise into slices as wide as the tuna's thickness and as long as the steak

3 tablespoons coarsely ground coriander seed (see Ming's Tip, page 107)

2 small heads frisée lettuce, washed, cored, and cut into bite-size pieces

Ming's Tip:

Wash the lettuce in the basket of a salad spinner plunged into a sinkful of cold water, drain it, and then spin dry. You can store the lettuce—or any lettuce you want to use later—in the basket in the fridge.

tofu greek salad

Greek salad is one of those classic dishes that travels far beyond its country of origin. As much as I enjoy it, I figured that there was a different, more refined way to approach it. My version is most deliciously notable for its substitution of firm tofu for the usual salty feta. Believe me, there's no flavor sacrifice, as I've also included fermented black beans and garlic in the dressing.

1. Heat a medium sauté pan over medium-high heat. Add ¼ cup of the oil and swirl to coat the bottom. When the oil is hot, add the scallion whites, garlic, and beans and sauté, stirring, until softened, about 1 minute. Add the tomatoes and sauté until softened, about 3 minutes.

2. In a medium bowl, combine the mustard and lemon juice, the remaining ¼ cup oil, the parsley and the olives. Add the tomato mixture and romaine lettuce, and toss gently to combine. Season with salt and pepper. Add the tofu and toss gently again. Garnish with the lemon zest and serve.

TO DRINK:
A crisp Sauvignon Blanc, like Sauvignon Republic Cellars from California

[Serves 4]

½ cup extra-virgin olive oil

1 bunch scallions, sliced thin, white and green parts separated

1 tablespoon minced garlic

1 tablespoon minced fermented black beans

1 pint cherry tomatoes, halved

2 tablespoons Dijon mustard

Juice and zest of 1 lemon

½ cup loosely packed flat-leaf parsley leaves

¼ cup pitted chopped Niçose olives

1 large head romaine, tough outer leaves removed, cored, halved, and cut widthwise into 1-inch pieces

Kosher salt and freshly ground black pepper

One 14-ounce package firm tofu, cut into ½-inch dice

TO DRINK:
An unoaked Chardonnay, like
Foxglove from California

[Serves 4]

6 slices bacon

3 ripe avocados, roughly chopped

1 bunch scallions, sliced thin, white and
green parts separated

¼ cup packed flat-leaf parsley leaves

Juice of 3 limes

Kosher salt and freshly ground black pepper

¼ cup extra-virgin olive oil

–

1 head iceberg lettuce, washed, cored, and
cut into 1-inch pieces, 1 cup set aside

3 tomatoes, cut into ¼-inch slices

3 hard-boiled eggs, sliced ¼ inch thick

2 cups frozen peas, rinsed in hot water and
drained, ¼ cup set aside for garnish

One 12-ounce package silken tofu, cut
lengthwise into ¼-inch slices

Ming's Tip:

If you can get really fresh peas,
by all means use them. Otherwise,
frozen peas work beautifully.

tofu green goddess salad

Layered salads were part of my growing up in Ohio. Though I don't recall any made with green goddess dressing—a tarragon- and anchovy-spiked mayonnaise blend—mayo was a constant. This lighter version features tofu in place of the mayo, plus avocado, which ensures creaminess. The salad is layered in a bowl and unmolded—a pretty, as well as mouthwatering, presentation.

1. In a medium skillet, cook the bacon over medium-low heat until crisp, about 8 minutes. Drain on paper towels, roughly chop, and set aside.

2. To make the dressing, combine the avocados, scallion whites, parsley and lime juice in a food processor and purée. Season with salt and pepper. With the processor running, drizzle in the oil. Adjust the seasoning, if necessary.

3. In a small bowl, combine the 1 cup lettuce with 2 tablespoons of the dressing, toss, and set aside. Reserve ¼ cup of the dressing for garnish.

4. To make the salad, in a large salad bowl layer as follows (seasoning with salt and pepper, and spooning on some of the larger quantity of dressing between the layers): tomatoes, eggs, peas, tofu, bacon, dressed and undressed lettuce. Press down gently with a hand or large spoon to compress, and refrigerate for 30 minutes.

5. Unmold the salad on a large round platter. Garnish with the reserved dressing, the scallion greens and reserved peas, and serve.

Acknowledgments

Both authors would like to thank Kyle Cathie, and US publisher and editor Anja Schmidt for her passion for perfection. Working with her has been a joy.

Ming Tsai

Many thanks to chefs Joanne O'Connell and Denise Swidey, who did an amazing job at a furious pace for this book. Thanks also to the entire Blue Ginger crew, led by Jonathan Taylor, Tom Woods, Jonathan Donoghue, Myron Chinn, and Mario Solls, and to Michele Fadden and Deanne Steffen. My gratitude as well to Blue Ginger managers Paula Taylor, Deborah Blish and Erika Staaf.

My thanks also for the great assistance provided by Jill Hardy and Lisa Falso—for their help with all logistics and props, not to mention the 5-Hour Energy shots! And gratitude to Melissa's/World Variety Produce, Inc., Captain Marden's Seafoods, T. F. Kinnealey & Co. and John Dewar and Company for their ongoing support and for providing their superior products for the shoot.

To the amazing photographer Antonis Achilleos, assisted by Christopher Coppa, many thanks for his beautiful, elegant photos.

Thanks also to Sandy Montag, my agent at IMG, for all you've done. And thanks to my writer extraordinaire, Arthur Boehm. This is our third book, Artie, but definitely not our last!

Arthur Boehm

Thanks, first, to Ming Tsai, for his wonderful food and the pleasure of writing about it this third time. Many thanks also to my agent, Joy Tutela of David Black Literary Agency, for her warmly attentive professionalism. Gratitude, too, to Lisa Falso for her generous help in preparing the recipes for publication. And many kisses to Tama Starr for her friendship and support in so many ways—then, now, and, with any luck, always.

THANKS

index